Burlington Books

Let's GO! 1

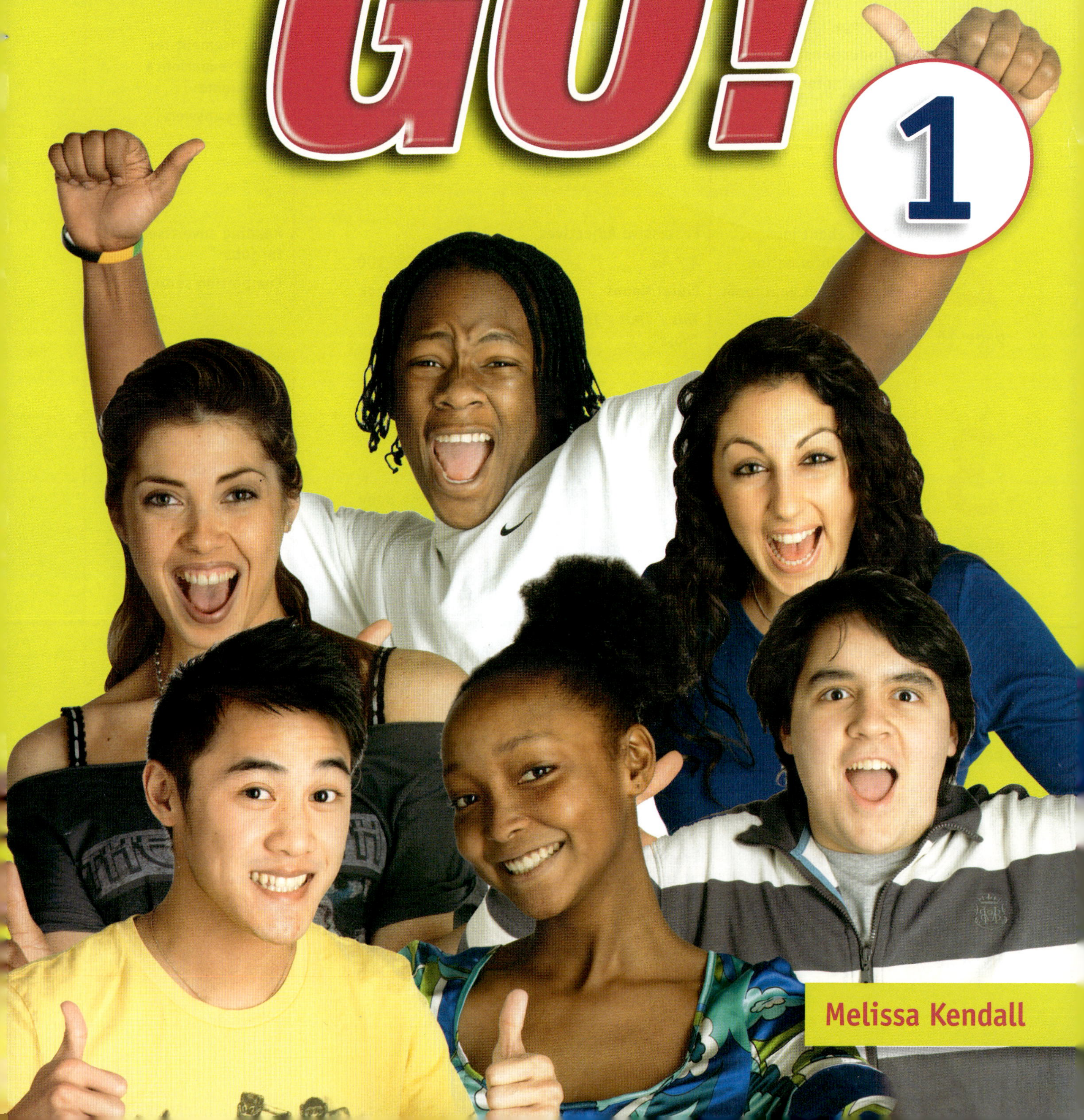

Melissa Kendall

Contents

Meet the characters !

EMILY

26 years old

from England

TEACHER

DESHI

18 years old

from China

STUDENT

HENRY

18 years old

from Nigeria

STUDENT

DANIELLE

19 years old

from France

STUDENT

CARI

18 years old

from Turkey

STUDENT

MARISA

19 years old

from Brazil

STUDENT

TONI

18 years old

from Spain

STUDENT

Introduction

Instrucciones

1 Mira en tu libro y busca un ejemplo de cada tipo de ejercicio. Anota el número de la página y el del ejercicio.

	Page (Página)	Exercise (Ejercicio)
1. Listen, read and repeat. (Escucha, lee y repite.)	8	1
2. Listen and complete the dialogue. (Escucha y completa el diálogo.)		
3. Listen again and check your answers. (Escucha de nuevo y comprueba las respuestas.)		
4. Practise with other students. (Practica con otros compañeros/as.)		
5. Write the answer. (Escribe la respuesta.)		
6. Read the grammar box. (Lee el cuadro de gramática.)		
7. Complete the sentences. (Completa las oraciones.)		
8. Answer the questions. (Responde a las preguntas.)		
9. Put the words in the correct order. (Pon las palabras en el orden correcto.)		
10. In pairs, change the words in colour. Act out the dialogue. (En parejas, cambiad las palabras en color y practicad el nuevo diálogo.)		

Inglés cotidiano

2 **Muchas palabras son iguales o parecidas en castellano y en inglés. Pon la palabra adecuada debajo de cada foto.**

telephone   menu   ~~ambulance~~   hamburger   bus   passport   hotel   taxi

1. ...ambulance...

2. ....

3. ....

4. ....

5. ....

6. ....

7. ....

8. ....

El abecedario

3 **Escucha, lee y repite.**

a	b	c	d	e	f	g	h	i	j	k	l	m
/eɪ/	/biː/	/siː/	/diː/	/iː/	/ef/	/dʒiː/	/eɪtʃ/	/aɪ/	/dʒeɪ/	/keɪ/	/el/	/em/

n	o	p	q	r	s	t	u	v	w	x	y	z
/en/	/əʊ/	/piː/	/kjuː/	/ɑː/	/es/	/tiː/	/juː/	/viː/	/ˈdʌbljuː/	/eks/	/waɪ/	/zed/

4 **A Escucha y lee.**

1. What's this in English?
2. It's a passport.
3. Can you spell it, please?
4. Yes, P-A-S-S-P-O-R-T.

B Deletrea las palabras del Ejercicio 2 a un compañero/a.

unit 1

What's your name?

1 **Listen, read and repeat.**

2 **Listen, read and repeat the greetings.**

1. Hello. / Hi.
2. Good morning.
3. Good afternoon.
4. Good evening.

3 **A Listen and complete the dialogues.**

EMILY: [1] Hello .... My name's Emily. What's your name?

TONI: My name's Toni.

EMILY: Good morning. My [2]........ Emily. What's your name?

CARI: I'm Cari.

EMILY: Good afternoon. [3]........ name's Emily.
What's [4]........ name?

DESHI: My name's Deshi.

EMILY: Good evening. I'm Emily. What's [5]........ .... ?

MARISA: [6]........ Marisa.

B Listen again and check your answers.

4 **Practise with another student.**

STUDENT 1: What's your name?

STUDENT 2: My name's / I'm ....

WORDS Numbers: 0-19

5 A Listen, read and repeat.

0	nought / oh	4	four	8	eight	12	twelve	16	sixteen
1	one	5	five	9	nine	13	thirteen	17	seventeen
2	two	6	six	10	ten	14	fourteen	18	eighteen
3	three	7	seven	11	eleven	15	fifteen	19	nineteen

B Listen and write the numbers you hear.

a. .... b. .... c. .... d. .... e. .... f. .... g. .... h. .... i. .... j. .... k. .... l. ....

6 A Write the answers in words.

1. six + three = ...nine........
2. seven + one = ...
3. eleven + two = ...
4. four - four = ...
5. eighteen - six = ...
6. ten - eight = ...
7. fourteen + five = ...
8. nineteen - thirteen = ...

B Listen and check your answers.

What's your ... ?

7 A Listen and read.

B Practise with another student.

8 A Listen, read and repeat.

RECEPTIONIST: Good morning. What's your name, please?

LUCY: Good morning. My name's Lucy Dalton.

RECEPTIONIST: What's your phone number, Ms Dalton?

LUCY: It's 020 8392 8561.

RECEPTIONIST: Thank you.

B Listen and complete the information below.

ALBANY HOTEL

REGISTRATION FORM

NAME: 1 ...Mark.............................

ADDRESS: 2 .... Baker ....
London

TELEPHONE NUMBER: 3 ...020.....................

C Listen again and check your answers.

GRAMMAR

9 **A** **Read the grammar box.**

To be		
Affirmative		
I **am**	>	I'**m**
you **are**	>	you'**re**
he **is**	>	he'**s**
she **is**	>	she'**s**
it **is**	>	it'**s**
we **are**	>	we'**re**
you **are**	>	you'**re**
they **are**	>	they'**re**

B **Complete the sentences with *am*, *is* or *are*.**

1. I ......*am*...... Deshi.
2. You .... Cari.
3. He .... Toni.
4. They .... students.
5. I .... fine, thanks.
6. We .... students.
7. Marisa .... a student.
8. It .... the school.

C **Write the sentences with contractions.**

1. I am Toni.
   I'm Toni...............................
2. She is at school.
   ....
3. It is 020 8392 8561.
   ....
4. You are Cari.
   ....
5. They are students.
   ....

Nice to meet you.

10 **Listen, read and repeat.**

1

2

3

11 A Listen and complete the dialogues.

DESHI: [1] ......Hi......, Emily. How are you?

EMILY: I'm [2] ...., thanks, Deshi. And you?

DESHI: I'm fine, thanks.

CARI: Henry, [3] .... is [4] .... friend, Danielle.

HENRY: [5] ...., Danielle.

DANIELLE: [6] ...., Henry. [7] .... to meet you. [8] .... are you from, Henry?

HENRY: I'm [9] .... Nigeria.

B Listen again and check your answers.

12 Practise with other students.

1. *STUDENT 1:* Hello, ... How are you?
   STUDENT 2: Fine, thanks, ... And you?
   STUDENT 1: Fine, thanks.
2. *STUDENT 1:* ...., this is ....
   STUDENT 2: Hello, ...
   STUDENT 3: Hello, ... Nice to meet you.
   STUDENT 2: Where are you from?
   STUDENT 3: I'm from ....

GRAMMAR

13 A Read the grammar box.

To be			
Negative			
I am **not**		> I'm **not**	
he / she / it	is **not**	> he / > she / > it	's **not**/isn't
you / we / they	are **not**	> you / > we / > they	're **not**/aren't

B Write the sentences in the negative. Use the full form.

1. It is a pencil.
   It is not a pencil.
2. Emily is French.
   ....
3. We are from France.
   ....
4. I am Mark.
   ....
5. You are a student.
   ....
6. Danielle and Henry are from Turkey.
   ....

C Write the sentences in B. Use contractions.

1. It's not a pencil. / It isn't a pencil.
2. ....
3. ....
4. ....
5. ....
6. ....

14 A Read the grammar box.

To be		
Questions		
I **am**	>	**Am** I … ?
he / she / it **is**	>	**Is** he … ?
	>	**Is** she … ?
	>	**Is** it … ?
you / we / they **are**	>	**Are** you … ?
	>	**Are** we … ?
	>	**Are** they … ?
Short Answers		
Yes, he **is.** / No, she**'s not.**		

B Put the words in the correct order.

1. he / Is / a / student / ?
   Is he a student?
2. you / from / Are / Turkey / ?
   ....
3. Toni / your / name / Is / ?
   ....
4. you / Are / a / teacher / ?
   ....
5. they / Are / Nigerian / ?
   ....
6. Marisa / China / from / Is / ?
   ....

WORDS The Classroom

15 A Listen, read and repeat.

chair   dictionary   pencil   desk   notebook   pen   ~~book~~   board

B Write the correct word using the pictures below.

1. It's a ....*book*.... .

2. It's a ....

3. It's a ....

4. It's a ....

5. It's a ....

6. It's a ....

7. It's a ....

8. It's a ....

C Listen and check your answers.

16 A Listen and read.

What's this?

It's a book.

B Work with a partner. Ask questions using the words from 15 A.

WORDS Countries and Nationalities

17 A Match the nationalities to the pictures. One nationality hasn't got a match. Circle it.

Nigerian Brazilian Chinese Turkish ~~English~~ French Spanish

1. This is J. K. Rowling.
   She's from England.
   She's ...English... .

2. This is Antonio Banderas.
   He's from Spain.
   He's ....

3. This is Manu Chao.
   He's from France.
   He's ....

4. This is Yao Ming.
   He's from China.
   He's ....

5. This is Ronaldinho.
   He's from Brazil.
   He's ....

6. This is Sade.
   She's from Nigeria.
   She's ....

B Listen and check your answers.

PRONUNCIATION

18 Listen and repeat.

1. I am English.
2. I'm English.
3. You are Turkish.
4. You're Turkish.
5. He is Chinese.
6. He's Chinese.

READING

19 A Read this advertisement.

B Answer the questions about the advertisement.

1. What's the name of the hotel?
   It's the ....
2. What's the name of the manager?
   His ....
3. What's the telephone number of the hotel?
   It's ....
4. What's the address of the hotel?
   It's ....

review

WORD LIST

board	Chinese	England	France	notebook	seventeen	thirteen
book	desk	English	French	nought / oh	six	three
Brazil	dictionary	fifteen	Nigeria	one	sixteen	Turkey
Brazilian	eight	five	Nigerian	pen	Spain	Turkish
chair	eighteen	four	nine	pencil	Spanish	twelve
China	eleven	fourteen	nineteen	seven	ten	two

VOCABULARY

1 **Look at the word list above and do the following exercises.**

1. List three things students take to school in their schoolbags.

........*book*........ ....

....

2. Complete with the correct numbers.

two, 1........................, six,
2........................, ten,
3........................, 4........................

3. Complete the chart.

Country	Nationality
China	
	Turkish
	Brazilian
England	

GRAMMAR

2 **Choose the correct answer.**

1. Deshi **is** / **are** Chinese.
2. My name **am** / **is** Emily.
3. I **am not** / **isn't** fourteen.
4. The teacher **isn't** / **aren't** Turkish.
5. My friends **is** / **are** students.
6. We **am** / **are** at school.

3 **Put the words in the correct order.**

1. you / Are / student / a / ?
   Are you a student?
2. Marisa / Nigerian / Is / ?
   ....
3. students / Are / they / ?
   ....
4. Toni / Brazil / from / Is / ?
   ....
5. Chinese / Henry / Are / and / Cari / ?
   ....

LISTENING

4 **A** **Listen and choose the correct answer.**

1. a. Thank you.
   b. I'm Marisa.
2. a. It's 12 Harrington Gardens.
   b. It's 020 8489 9231.
3. a. It's a book.
   b. I'm fine, thanks.
4. a. Yes, I am.
   b. No, she isn't.
5. a. He's from Brazil.
   b. Good afternoon!
6. a. I'm a student.
   b. Nice to meet you.

B **Listen and check your answers.**

LET'S GO: YOUR TURN

1 Listen and read the dialogue.

RECEPTIONIST: Good afternoon. My name is **Brenda**. What's your name?

KATE: My name's **Kate**.

RECEPTIONIST: Nice to meet you. Where are you from, **Kate**?

KATE: I'm from **Turkey**.

RECEPTIONIST: Are you from **Istanbul**?

KATE: Yes, I am.

RECEPTIONIST: What's your address in London?

KATE: It's **13 Pimlico Road**.

RECEPTIONIST: And what's your phone number, **Kate**?

KATE: It's **020 8419 8607**.

RECEPTIONIST: Thank you.

2 In pairs, change the words in colour. Act out your new dialogue.

3 Ask three students the following questions and write their answers.

	Name	What's your phone number?	Where are you from?
1			
2			
3			

DID YOU KNOW?

England is one of the four countries in the United Kingdom. The other three countries are: Northern Ireland, Scotland and Wales. Look at the chart.

	England	N.Ireland	Scotland	Wales
Population	50.8 million	1.7 million	5.1 million	3 million
Capital City	London	Belfast	Edinburgh	Cardiff
Languages	English	English Irish Gaelic	English Scottish Gaelic	English Welsh

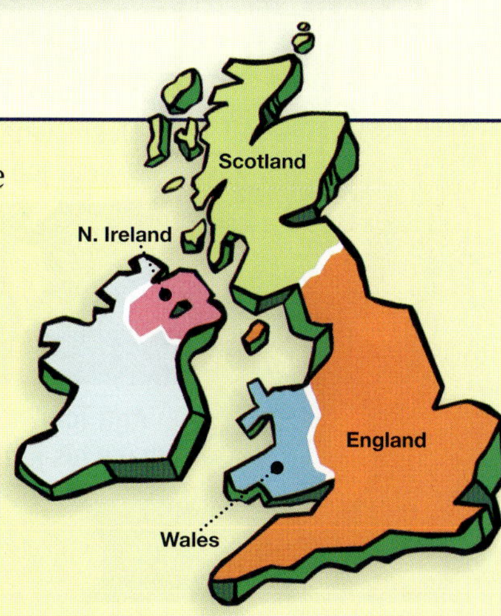

What's your job?

1 **Listen, read and repeat.**

WORDS Jobs

2 **A** **Complete the sentences with the correct job.**

housekeeper receptionist doctor ~~waiter~~ porter electrician shop assistant cook

1. What's his job? He's a ....*waiter*.... .
2. What's his job? He's an ....
3. What's her job? She's a ....
4. What's her job? She's a ....
5. What's her job? She's a ....
6. What's his job? He's a ....
7. What's her job? She's a ....
8. What's her job? She's a ....

B **Listen and check your answers.**

3 **Practise with another student.**

STUDENT 1: What's Toni's job?

STUDENT 2: He's a ....

GRAMMAR

4 A Read the grammar box.

Personal Pronouns		Possessive Adjectives
I	>	**my**
you	>	**your**
he	>	**his**
she	>	**her**
it	>	**its**
we	>	**our**
you	>	**your**
they	>	**their**
He is a student. This is **his** book.		

B Complete the sentences with the correct possessive adjectives.

1. Hello! ....My.......... name's Emily.
2. What's .... job? Is he a waiter?
3. Are you a porter? What's .... job?
4. Hello! .... name's Marisa. What's .... name?
5. This is Danielle. .... boyfriend is a cook.

5 A Read the grammar box.

A / An
a before consonants: **a** waiter **an** before *a, e, i, o, u*: **an** electrician

B Write *a* or *an*.

1. ....an.......... electrician
2. .... doctor
3. .... English teacher
4. .... Chinese man
5. .... girlfriend
6. .... office
7. .... book

WORDS Numbers: 20-100

6 Listen, read and repeat.

20 twenty	25 twenty-five
21 twenty-one	26 twenty-six
22 twenty-two	27 twenty-seven
23 twenty-three	28 twenty-eight
24 twenty-four	29 twenty-nine

7 A Listen, read and repeat.

30 thirty	70 seventy
40 forty	80 eighty
50 fifty	90 ninety
60 sixty	100 one hundred

B Listen and circle the number you hear.

a. 14 / 40	e. 18 / 80
b. 17 / 70	f. 15 / 50
c. 13 / 30	g. 19 / 90
d. 16 / 60	h. 12 / 20

How old are you?

8 A Listen and read.

B Practise with another student.

9 A Listen and complete the dialogue.

DESHI: Good morning. My name [1] ....*is*.......... Deshi Lee.

RECEPTIONIST: Good [2] .... , Deshi. What's [3] .... address, please?

DESHI: It's the Albany Hotel, [4] .... Brook Road.

RECEPTIONIST: And [5] .... your telephone number, please?

DESHI: [6] .... phone number is 020 4298 4300.

RECEPTIONIST: How old [7] .... you, Deshi?

DESHI: I [8] .... eighteen.

RECEPTIONIST: Deshi, [9] .... is Dr Grant.

DR GRANT: Nice to meet [10] .... , Deshi.

B Listen again and check your answers.

10 A Listen and complete the information.

DR GRANT'S SURGERY

PATIENT FILE

Name:	
Address:	
Telephone:	
Age:	
Nationality:	
Job:	

B Listen again and check your answers.

This is my room.

11 Listen, read and repeat.

12 A Listen and complete the dialogue.

DANIELLE: Toni, that's Deshi and Henry's [1] ....*room*.......... and this is [2] .... room.

TONI: Danielle, are these [3] .... CDs?

DANIELLE: [4] .... , they're not. They're Cari's CDs.

TONI: What's [5] .... , Danielle?

DANIELLE: Oh, [6] .... a pen [7] .... France.

B Listen again and check your answers.

GRAMMAR

13 A Read the grammar box.

Plural Nouns
1 book – 2 book**s**
1 dictionary – 2 dictionar**ies**

B Write about the pictures.

1. .... five books ....

2. ....

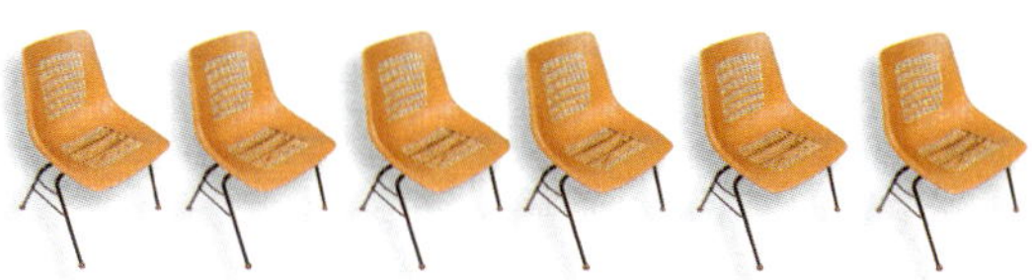

3. ....

4. ....

5. ....

14 A Read the grammar box.

This / That / These / Those

B Complete the sentences with *This* or *That*.

1. ...... That ...... is my chair.
2. .... is my dictionary.
3. .... is my desk.
4. .... is my friend.

C Write the sentences in the plural.

1. That waiter is Nigerian.
   Those waiters are Nigerian.
2. This is a Spanish dictionary.
   ....
3. This porter is from England.
   ....
4. That student is Turkish.
   ....
5. What is this?
   ....

PRONUNCIATION

15 Listen, read and repeat. Pay attention to the stressed words in colour.

1. What's your name? 2. How are you? 3. Fine, thanks. 4. This is a desk.

WORDS Days of the Week

16 A Listen, read and repeat.

1. Monday 2. Tuesday 3. Wednesday 4. Thursday 5. Friday 6. Saturday 7. Sunday

B Listen and read.

What day is it today?

It's Monday.

C Practise with a partner.

17 A Read the diary.

B Where is Marisa? Use the diary to complete the sentences.

1. On ....Sunday...... , Marisa is at home.
2. On .... , she is at the doctor.
3. On .... and .... , she is at work.
4. On .... , she is at a cooking lesson.
5. On .... , she is at a restaurant with friends.
6. On .... , she is at an English lesson.

C Listen and check your answers.

READING

18 A Read the advertisements.

B Match the people to the advertisements in A.

	Celine Chevallier	Alberto Romero	Carmen Ortega	Janet Wilson
AGE	18	18	16	17
JOB	student, receptionist	student, waiter	student, babysitter	student, shop assistant
NATIONALITY	French	Spanish	Brazilian	English

1. Advertisement ...1... is for ...Janet... because ...she's a shop assistant....
2. Advertisement .... is for .... because ....
3. ....
4. ....

LANGUAGE PRACTICE pages 76-79

review

WORD LIST

address	doctor	girlfriend	ninety	shop assistant	Tuesday
age	eighty	housekeeper	one hundred	sixty	twenty
babysitter	electrician	job	porter	Sunday	waiter
because	fifty	Monday	receptionist	thirty	Wednesday
boyfriend	forty	nationality	Saturday	Thursday	
cook	Friday	new	seventy	today	

VOCABULARY

1 **Look at the word list above and do the following exercises.**

1. List six jobs.

babysitter ....

....

....

2. Write the answers in words.

a. 10 + 10 = ...

b. 20 + 20 = ...

c. 70 - 20 = ...

d. 50 + 40 = ...

3. Complete the days of the week.

1........................, Tuesday,
2........................, 3........................,
Friday, 4........................, Sunday.

GRAMMAR

2 **Choose the correct answer.**

1. Hello! **My** / **Your** name is Alex. I'm **a** / **an** electrician.
2. I'm **a** / **an** receptionist. What's **its** / **your** job, Tom?
3. Kate is **a** / **an** student. **His** / **Her** books are here.
4. Linda and Peter are students. These are **their** / **our** books.

3 **Write *this, that, these* or *those* under the correct pictures.**

1

those

2
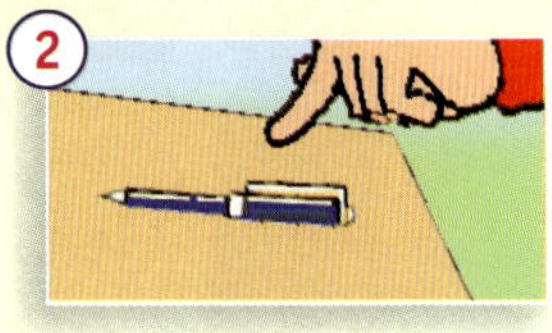
....

3
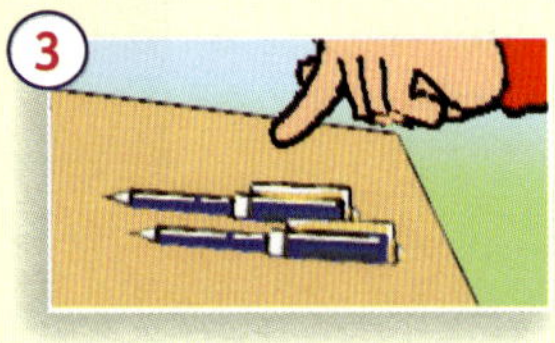
....

4

....

LISTENING

4 **A Listen and choose the correct answer.**

1. a. I'm a receptionist.
   b. I'm French.
2. a. He's a waiter.
   b. She's a doctor
3. a. I'm fine.
   b. I'm eighteen years old.
4. a. It's 24 Baker Street.
   b. It's 020 7549 8371.
5. a. It's a chair.
   b. Yes, they are.
6. a. It's Thursday.
   b. It's a book.

B Listen and check your answers.

LET'S GO: YOUR TURN

1 **Listen and read the dialogue.**

TEACHER: **Rachel**, how old are you?
RACHEL: I'm **17** years old.
TEACHER: What's your address?
RACHEL: It's **88 Gold Street**.
TEACHER: What's your **father's** job, **Rachel**?
RACHEL: **He's a doctor**.
TEACHER: And your **mother**? What's **her** job?
RACHEL: She's **an electrician**.

2 **In pairs, change the words in colour. Act out your new dialogue.**

3 **Ask three students the following questions and write their answers.**

	Name	How old are you?	What's your address?
1			
2			
3			

DID YOU KNOW?

People in England are from many different countries and cultures.
Today, 30% of people in London are originally from Asia, Africa, China or the Caribbean.

unit 3

Have you got any children?

1 **Listen, read and repeat.**

2 **A** **Listen and complete the dialogue.**

CARI: Marisa, 1.......this....... is my mother, Deniz Tarik.

MARISA: 2..................... to meet you, Mrs Tarik.

MRS TARIK: Where 3..................... you from, Marisa?

MARISA: I'm 4..................... Brazil.

MRS TARIK: Have 5..................... got a boyfriend?

MARISA: No, 6..................... .

B **Listen again and check your answers.**

3 **Practise with another student.**

STUDENT 1: Have you got a boyfriend / girlfriend?

STUDENT 2: Yes, I have. / No, I haven't.

WORDS The Family

4 **A Listen, read and repeat.**

husband		brother	
wife		sister	
father	parents	uncle	
mother	parents	aunt	
child		grandfather	grandparents
son	children	grandmother	grandparents
daughter	children	grandchild	
		grandchildren	

B Look at the pictures.

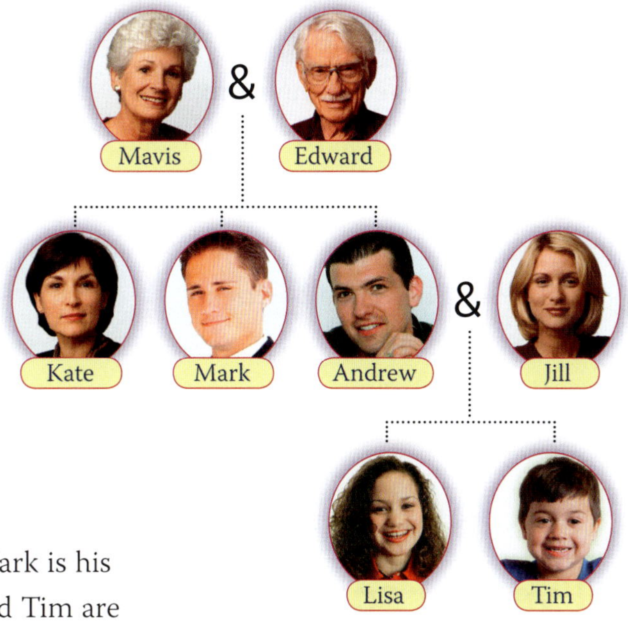

C Complete the text according to B.

This is Andrew. Kate is his 1...................... and Mark is his 2...................... . Jill is his 3...................... . Lisa and Tim are his 4...................... . Mavis and Edward are his 5...................... and 6...................... . Lisa and Tim are their 7...................... . Lisa and Tim have got an 8...................... and an 9...................... . Their names are Kate and Mark.

GRAMMAR

5 **A Read the grammar box.**

Have got			
Affirmative		**Negative**	
I / you / we / they **have got**	I / you / we / they **'ve got**	I / you / we / they **have not got**	I / you / we / they **haven't got**
he / she / it **has got**	he / she / it **'s got**	he / she / it **has got**	he / she / it **hasn't got**
Questions		**Short Answers**	
Have you **got** a girlfriend? **Has** she **got** any brothers?		Yes, I **have**. No, she **hasn't**.	

B Complete the sentences with *have got* or *has got*.

1. I ......have got...... two sisters.
2. Mark .... a son.
3. We .... one brother.
4. They .... two uncles.
5. Alice .... two children.
6. You .... grandparents.

C **Write the sentences in the negative. Use contractions.**

1. He's got two sisters.
   He hasn't got two sisters.
2. We've got three brothers.
   ....
3. I've got a new girlfriend.
   ....
4. She's got a boyfriend.
   ....
5. They've got a Spanish dictionary.
   ....

D **Complete the questions with *Have ... got* or *Has ... got*.**

1. ...Have... you ...got... a sister?
2. .... Marisa .... a boyfriend?
3. .... Mr and Mrs Tarik .... any grandchildren?
4. .... Toni .... a girlfriend?
5. .... you .... a job?
6. .... Simon .... any children?
7. .... they .... a dictionary?

I've got some photos.

6 **Listen, read and repeat.**

7 A Listen and complete the dialogue.

EMILY: Look, these are my [1]....children...., Michael and Linda.

MRS TARIK: Oh, [2]...................... beautiful! They've got red hair! [3]...................... old are they?

EMILY: Michael's two and Linda's [4]...................... . Has Cari got [5]...................... brothers or sisters?

MRS TARIK: Yes, she [6]...................... . Her brother's name is Ali. But I [7]...................... got a photo here.

B Listen again and check your answers.

GRAMMAR

8 A Read the grammar box.

Countable Nouns
We can count these nouns. We can use these nouns in the singular and plural. **an** uncle, **two** uncles **a** child, **two** children

Uncountable Nouns
We can't count these nouns. We can't use these nouns in the plural. **some homework** NOT ~~homeworks~~

B Complete the phrases with *a*, *an* or *some*.

1. ....a......... taxi
2. .... coffee
3. .... aunt
4. .... popcorn
5. .... pen
6. .... water
7. .... girlfriend
8. .... tea

9 A Read the grammar box.

Some / Any
Affirmative
She's got **some** pens.
Negative
He hasn't got **any** water.
Questions
Have you got **any** children?

B Complete the sentences with *some* or *any*.

1. I've got ....some....... bananas.
2. Have you got .... brothers?
3. You haven't got .... coffee.
4. We've got .... money.
5. Have they got .... children?
6. I haven't got .... homework.

10 A Read the grammar box.

Saxon Genitive	
These are Cari**'s** parents. This is the teacher**'s** book.	**BUT:** This is James**'** girlfriend. These are the teacher**s'** books. This is Susie and Lisa**'s** grandfather.

B Look at Liz's family and complete the sentences.

1. Thomas is ......Liz's...... husband.
2. Liz is .... wife.
3. Ann is .... sister.
4. Dan is .... brother.
5. Liz is .... and .... mother.

PRONUNCIATION

11 Listen and repeat.

1. husband 2. have 3. brother 4. blue 5. five 6. book

WORDS Colours

12 Listen, read and repeat.

red grey blue black green white
pink brown yellow purple orange

WORDS Parts of the Body

13 Listen, read and repeat.

14 A Look at the pictures and complete the sentences.

1 

2 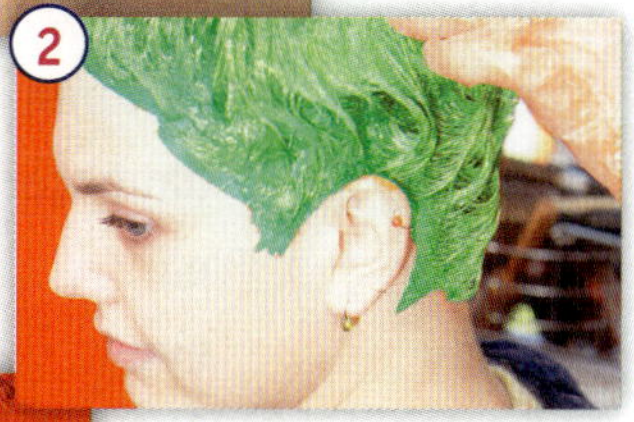

3 

4 

1. What colour are his eyes? His eyes are ......blue...... .
2. What colour is her hair? Her hair is ....
3. What colour is his nose? His nose is ....
4. What colour are its ears? Its ears are ....

B Listen and check your answers.

C Circle the word that doesn't belong.

1. eye • ear • (leg) • mouth
2. finger • nose • hand • arm
3. head • toe • foot • leg

D Write a description of yourself.

I have got .... hair and .... eyes.

I have got my ....'s hair and my ....'s eyes.

READING

15 A Read this e-mail.

To: sophia_t@mymail.com

From: marisa_o@emessenger.com

Subject: Hi from London

Hi, Sophia!

London is fantastic! I love the hotel programme. My English teacher is great. Her name is Emily and she's from Manchester. Emily's husband is an electrician and they've got two beautiful children. Their son, Michael, is two and his sister, Linda, is one. They've got red hair and blue eyes!

I've got a new friend. Her name is Danielle and she is French. She's got a boyfriend. His name is Paul and he's a waiter.

What's new? Please write!

Love,

Marisa

B Correct the mistake in each sentence.

1. Emily's husband is a doctor. ......Emily's husband is an electrician......
2. Emily and her husband haven't got any children. ....
3. Linda has got two brothers. ....
4. Danielle is Emily's friend. ....
5. Danielle is English. ....
6. Danielle hasn't got a boyfriend. ....

review

WORD LIST

arm	brown	father	grandparents	leg	parents	uncle
aunt	child	finger	green	married	pink	What's new?
beautiful	children	foot	grey	mother	purple	white
black	daughter	grandchild	hair	mouth	red	wife
blue	ear	grandchildren	hand	nose	sister	yellow
body	eye	grandfather	head	on holiday	son	
brother	family	grandmother	husband	orange	toe	

VOCABULARY

1 **Look at the word list above and do the following exercises.**

1. Complete the chart with six family members.

Women	Men
daughter	

2. Write the correct colours.

a. red + white = ...

b. black + white = ...

c. yellow + blue = ...

d. blue + red = ...

3. Complete the chart with six parts of the body.

Head	Body

GRAMMAR

2 **A Complete the sentences with *have got* or *has got*.**

1. I ...have got... black hair.
2. My sister .... blue eyes.
3. .... Jim .... his father's nose?
4. The children .... beautiful eyes.
5. .... you .... any aunts?

B Write the sentences in the negative.

1. You've got my book.
   You haven't got my book.
2. Marisa and I have got new dictionaries.
   ....
3. Toni has got a girlfriend.
   ....

3 **Choose the correct answer.**

1. Have you got **a** / **any** homework?
2. I've got **some** / **any** money.
3. We haven't got **some** / **any** water.
4. Has Marisa got **some** / **any** brothers?
5. Have you got your **mother's** / **mothers'** eyes?
6. This is **Jame's** / **James'** brother.

LISTENING

4 **A Listen and choose the correct answer.**

1. a. Yes, I am. b. Emily is my sister.
2. a. These are my parents. b. No, I haven't.
3. a. Yes, she has. b. She's got black hair.
4. a. Yes, I'm fine. b. I've got two sisters.
5. a. It's from China. b. It's purple.

B Listen and check your answers.

LET'S GO: YOUR TURN

1 Listen and read the dialogue.

LINDA: Where are you from, **Dan**?

DAN: I'm from **Paris**. What about you? Where are you from?

LINDA: I'm from **London**. Have you got any brothers or sisters?

DAN: Yes, I have. I've got one brother and one sister.

LINDA: Have **they** got your **blue eyes**?

DAN: My brother has got my blue eyes, but my sister hasn't. **She's** got green eyes and **red hair**.

2 In pairs, change the words in colour. Act out your new dialogue.

3 Ask three students the following questions and write their answers.

	Name	Have you got any brothers or sisters?	What colour are your eyes?
1			
2			
3			

DID YOU KNOW?

Look at the family tree of the British royal family. Who in the British royal family has got the same name as a Spanish chain of clothes shops?

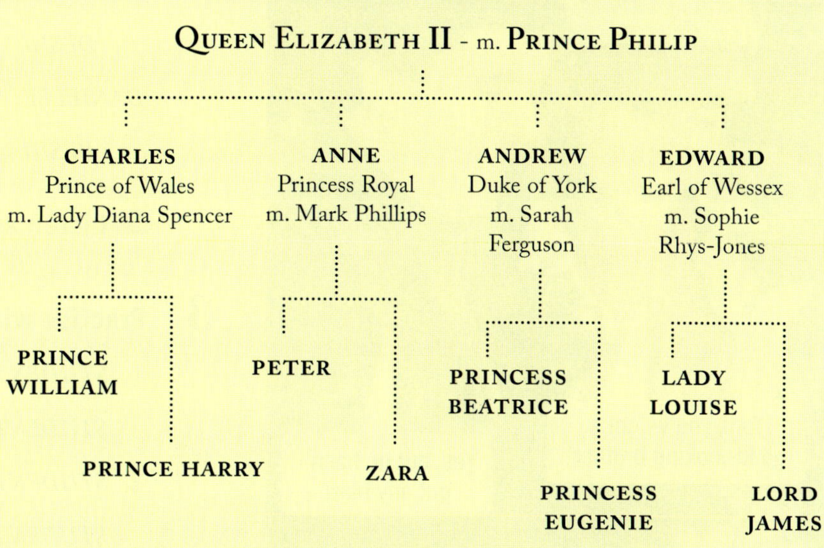

unit 4

She's beautiful!

1 **Listen, read and repeat.**

2 **A Listen and complete the dialogue.**

DESHI:	This is 1 ....my......... mother.
DANIELLE:	Wow! She's got very long 2 .... !
DESHI:	Yes, she has. And this is my 3 ....
DANIELLE:	He's very 4 ....
DESHI:	And very 5 .... too.
DANIELLE:	Deshi, you have got a beautiful family.
DESHI:	6 .... !

B Listen again and check your answers.

3 **Practise with other students.**

1. *STUDENT 1:* Are you tall?
   STUDENT 2: Yes, I am. / No, I'm not.
2. *STUDENT 1:* Have you got long hair?
   STUDENT 2: Yes, I have. / No, I haven't.

WORDS Adjectives

4 **Listen, read and repeat.**

1. He's tall.
   She's short.

2. He's good-looking.
   She's beautiful.

3. They're ugly.
   He's got big ears.

4. She's got blonde hair.
   He's got dark hair.

5. He's old.
   She's young.

6. They're middle-aged.
   She's got small hands.

7. He's got long hair.
   She's got short hair.

8. He's thin.
   She's fat.

5 **A Tick (✓) the sentences that are true for you.**

- ☐ I'm tall.
- ☐ I'm short.
- ☐ I've got blond(e) hair.
- ☐ I've got brown eyes.
- ☐ I've got green eyes.
- ☐ I'm middle-aged.
- ☐ I've got blue eyes.
- ☐ I've got long hair.
- ☐ I've got dark hair.
- ☐ I'm young.

B Tell the class about yourself.

GRAMMAR

6 **A Read the grammar box.**

Word Order
Adjective + noun: Emily has got **beautiful children**.
Adjective after verb *to be*: He **is old**.

B Put the words in the correct order.

1. dark / got / She's / hair
   She's got dark hair.
2. got / a / sister / beautiful / They've
   ....
3. are / eyes / blue / Tom's
   ....
4. got / ears / big / She's
   ....
5. young / Kate / is
   ....
6. an / It's / book / English
   ....

How much ... ?

7 **Listen, read and repeat.**

8 **A Listen and complete the dialogue.**

MRS TARIK: Look! There's a snake. Isn't it [1] ....*long*.... !

DANIELLE: Oooh! [2] .... long and ugly!

CARI: No, it [3] .... It's beautiful. Excuse me, have you got [4] .... King snakes?

DANIELLE: Cari! A snake?

SALES ASSISTANT: Yes, there are [5] .... King snakes here.

CARI: How much is [6] .... snake?

SALES ASSISTANT: It's £60.

DANIELLE: OK, now let's go and look at [7] .... clothes.

B Listen again and check your answers.

WORDS Pets

9 **A Listen, read and repeat.**

B Say the animals. Use the pictures in A.

1. I'm old and thin. I'm brown.
   What am I?
   ......the dog......
2. I'm fat and black.
   What am I?
   ....
3. I'm orange.
   What am I?
   ....
4. I'm white. I've got long ears and pink eyes.
   What am I?
   ....
5. I'm small, white and brown.
   What am I?
   ....
6. I'm young and white.
   What am I?
   ....
7. I'm long and green.
   What am I?
   ....
8. I'm young. I'm grey, black and white.
   What am I?
   ....

C Listen and check your answers.

PRONUNCIATION

10 **Listen, read and repeat.**

1. I've got two white cats. (↘)
2. Have you got a hamster? (↗)
3. She is beautiful. (↘)
4. Are there any snakes here? (↗)
5. Is he tall? (↗)
6. Where is your puppy? (↘)

GRAMMAR

11 **A** **Read the grammar box.**

There is / There are
Affirmative
There is + singular countable nouns / uncountable nouns **There is** a chair in the room. **There is** some money on the table. *There are* + plural nouns **There are** some chairs here.
Negative
There isn't a chair in the room. **There isn't** any money on the table. **There aren't** any chairs in the room.
Questions
Is there a chair in the room? Yes, **there is.** / No, **there isn't.** **Is there** any money on the table? Yes, **there is.** / No, **there isn't.** **Are there** any chairs in the room? Yes, **there are.** / No, **there aren't.**

B **Look at the picture below. Complete the sentences with *There is, There are, There isn't* or *There aren't*.**

1. There is a desk.
2. .... some students.
3. .... some pens.
4. .... a red chair.
5. .... some water.
6. .... any dictionaries.

C **Complete the questions with *Is there* or *Are there*. Then answer the questions. Make them true for you.**

1. Is there a French student in your class?
   Yes, there is. / No, there isn't.
2. .... any Spanish students in your class?
   ....
3. .... a shop on your street?
   ....
4. .... a dictionary on your desk?
   ....

12 **A** **Read the grammar box.**

How much / How many
How much + uncountable nouns **How much** homework is there today? We also use *how much* to ask the price of something. **How much** are these chairs? *How many* + plural nouns **How many** cats have you got?

B Complete the questions with *How much* or *How many*.

1. ...How much... tea is there?
2. .... sisters have you got?
3. .... people are there in your family?
4. .... is this book?
5. .... students are there in your class?
6. .... money have you got?

READING

13 A Match the names to the photos.

..3.. King Juan Carlos ...... Robbie Williams ...... Penélope Cruz
...... Queen Elizabeth ...... Catherine Zeta-Jones

B Match the descriptions to the pictures. There is one extra picture.

FAMOUS PEOPLE

A ☐ *He's from England and he's a singer. He's got green eyes. He's very good-looking. He hasn't got a wife or any children.*

B ☐ *She's a beautiful actress. She has got long, black hair and brown eyes . Her husband is an American actor. He isn't young. She's got a son and a daughter.*

C ☐ *She is from England. She's got short, grey hair. She's old. There is a picture of this English woman on the money of her country.*

D ☐ *There are many beautiful actresses in Hollywood. This beautiful actress is also Spanish. She's got long, brown hair. She's got two dogs.*

C Write a description for the extra picture.

....

....

....

....

....

....

I live in ...

1 **Listen, read and repeat.**

2 **A** **Listen and complete the dialogue.**

EMILY: Where do you live in France, Danielle?

DANIELLE: I live in a 1 ....flat.... in Paris.

EMILY: Where do 2 .... live, Toni?

TONI: I live in Barcelona. I live in a small 3 ....

EMILY: Cari 4 .... here today. Where does she live?

DANIELLE: Cari 5 .... in a flat in Istanbul. It's very nice. It's got a 6 .... kitchen and dining room.

B **Listen again and check your answers.**

3 **Practise with another student.**

STUDENT 1: Where do you live?

STUDENT 2: I live in a flat / house.

GRAMMAR

4 **A** **Read the grammar box.**

Present Simple			
I you we they	live	he she it	live**s**

B **Complete the sentences with *work / works* or *like / likes*.**

1. Paul ......likes...... his girlfriend, Danielle.
2. Toni .... at the hotel.
3. Emily and David .... in London.
4. Cari and Deshi .... Chinese food.
5. We .... in the city.
6. Deshi .... every day.
7. Marisa .... her job.
8. I .... in the evening.

WORDS Rooms of the House

5 **A** **Listen, read and repeat.**

1

bedroom

2

bathroom

3

kitchen

4

living room

5

dining room

6

garage

7

toilet

8

garden

B **Look at the picture below and answer these questions.**

1. Where's Jack? He's in the bedroom.
2. Where's Kevin? ....
3. Where are Mr and Mrs Clark?

   ....
4. Where's Lucy? ....
5. Where's Ann? ....
6. Where's Rob? ....

It's OK, but ...

6 **Listen, read and repeat.**

7 **A Listen and complete the dialogue.**

CARI: Here's a nice 1 ....rug.......... for our bedroom. Do you 2 .... it, Danielle?

DANIELLE: It's OK, but look! I like 3 .... rug! Do you like it?

CARI: I like the rug, but the 4 .... isn't nice. Look! This rug is yellow and 5 .... room is yellow, too.

DANIELLE: Yes, but it's an 6 .... rug.

B Listen again and check your answers.

WORDS Furniture

8 **A Listen, read and repeat.**

1. bed

2. sofa

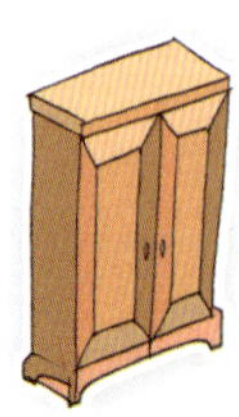
3. cupboard

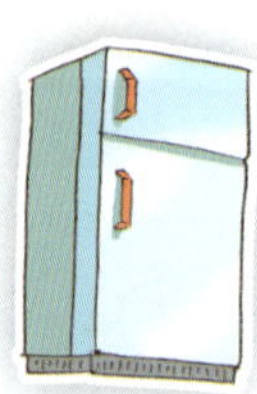
4. fridge

5. cooker

6. bookshelves

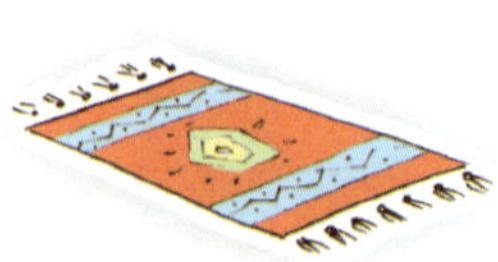
7. rug

8. lamp

9. poster

10. table

B Write the words from Exercise 8 A in the correct group. You can use some words more than once.

bedroom	dining room	living room	kitchen
bed			

WORDS Ordinal Numbers: 1st-12th

9 **A** Listen, read and repeat.

1st	first	**4th**	fourth	**7th**	seventh	**10th**	tenth
2nd	second	**5th**	fifth	**8th**	eighth	**11th**	eleventh
3rd	third	**6th**	sixth	**9th**	ninth	**12th**	twelfth

B Where are the items in the shop? Read the sign and write sentences about some of the items.

1. *The rugs are on the first floor.*
2. *The* ....
3. ....
4. ....
5. ....
6. ....
7. ....
8. ....

C Listen and read.

Where are the beds?

The beds are on the fifth floor.

D Work with another student. Ask questions using the sign.

PRONUNCIATION

10 Listen and repeat. Pay attention to the stressed syllable in colour.

1. garden 2. toilet 3. bedroom 4. table 5. cupboard

review

WORD LIST

bathroom	cupboard	first	garage	like	second	tenth
bed	dining room	flat	garden	living room	seventh	third
bedroom	eighth	floor	house	ninth	sixth	toilet
bookshelves	eleventh	fourth	kitchen	poster	sofa	twelfth
cooker	fifth	fridge	lamp	rug	table	

VOCABULARY

1 **Look at the word list above and do the following exercises.**

1. Complete the puzzle. Look at the clues below.

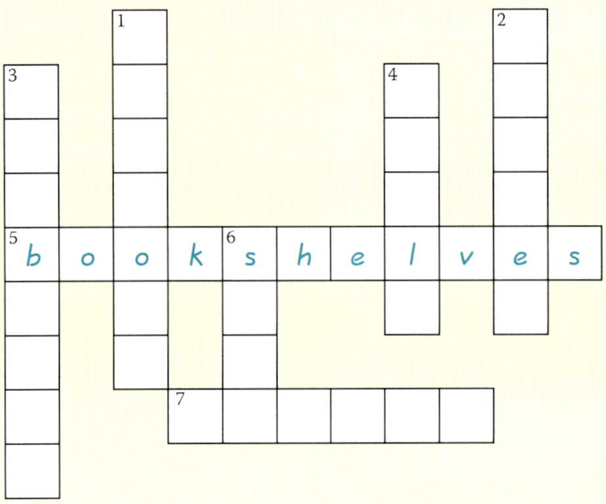

ACROSS ▶

5. You put books on them.
7. It's a "room" for a car.

DOWN ▼

1. Your bed is in it.
2. It's in the kitchen.
3. You put clothes in it.
4. You eat dinner on this.
6. You sit on it in the living room.

2. Complete with ordinal numbers.

first, 1..................... , third,
2..................... , 3..................... , sixth,
4..................... , 5..................... , ninth,
6..................... , eleventh, 7.....................

GRAMMAR

2 **Complete the sentences with the verbs in brackets. Use the Present Simple.**

1. We ....live......... (live) in France.
2. Emily .... (teach) the students.
3. Danielle and Cari .... (work) in the hotel.
4. Toni ....(go) to work every day.
5. Deshi .... (study) computers.

3 **Complete the sentences with the correct words.**

books ~~coffee~~ listening buying

1. Cari likes .....coffee..... , not tea.
2. Danielle likes .... clothes.
3. Toni likes history ....
4. Marisa likes .... to jazz music.

LISTENING

4 **A Listen and choose the correct answer.**

1. a. I live in a flat. b. I like London.
2. a. Yes, it's very big. b. Yes, it's ugly.
3. a. He likes music. b. He's in the bathroom.
4. a. It's in the garage. b. Sorry, I don't.
5. a. They're on the fourth floor. b. They're on the rug.

B Listen and check your answers.

LET'S GO: YOUR TURN

1 **Listen and read the dialogue.**

SANDRA: Where do you live, **Tom**?

TOM: I live in a **house** in **London**.

SANDRA: Do you like it?

TOM: **Yes**, I **do**. The bedrooms are **big** and the **garden** is **beautiful**. Where do you live, **Sandra**?

SANDRA: I live in a **flat** in **the centre of London**. It's **great**.

2 **In pairs, change the words in colour. Act out your new dialogue.**

3 **Ask three students the following questions and write their answers.**

	Name	Where do you live?	What colours do you like?
1			
2			
3			

DID YOU KNOW?

In Britain, 80% of people live in houses and only 20% live in flats. British houses are often small. The average house is 85 square metres. The British build their houses with red bricks. They like having a garden.

unit 6

He always goes to bed late.

1 Listen, read and repeat.

2

A Listen and complete the dialogue.

EMILY: Danielle and Henry, the 1......lesson...... starts at half past nine, 2...................... quarter to ten!

DANIELLE: I'm sorry 3...................... late, Emily.

HENRY: I'm 4...................... I'm late, too.

DESHI: 5...................... you OK, Danielle?

DANIELLE: 6...................... , but I'm tired.

HENRY: You're tired! What about 7......................? I go to bed at two o'clock in the 8......................!

EMILY: OK, everyone. Let's start the 9...................... .

B Listen again and check your answers.

3 Practise with another student.

1. *STUDENT 1:* Do you start school early?
   STUDENT 2: Yes, I do. / No, I don't.
2. *STUDENT 1:* Do you finish school late?
   STUDENT 2: Yes, I do. / No, I don't.

GRAMMAR

4 **A** **Read the grammar box.**

Adverbs of Frequency				
0%				100%
never	sometimes	often	usually	always

Adverbs of frequency usually come before the main verb.
I **never** have breakfast. He **sometimes** works late.

B **Tick (✓) the column which is right for you.**

How often do you ...?	never	sometimes	often	usually	always
1. read a book					
2. listen to music					
3. go to a restaurant					

C **Tell the class your answers.**

WORDS Telling the Time

5 **A** **Listen, read and repeat.**

1. It's five o'clock.

2. It's ten past five.

3. It's quarter past five.

4. It's half past five.

5. It's quarter to six.

6. It's ten to six.

7. It's midday.

8. It's midnight.

B **Look at the pictures and write the times.**

1. It's *ten past four* .
2. It's ....
3. It's ....
4. It's ....
5. It's ....
6. It's ....
7. It's ....
8. It's ....

C **Listen and read.**

D **Practise with a partner.**

unit 7

Who can sing?

1 **Listen, read and repeat.**

2 **A** **Listen and complete the dialogue.**

CARI: Hi, Henry. Listen. Marisa, Danielle and I want to start a rock [1] ......group...... .

HENRY: Great! I can [2] .... the guitar and I can [3] .... , too! Can I be in the group?

CARI: OK. Can you [4] .... at five o'clock? We want to practise for Deshi's party.

HENRY: No, I'm sorry. I [5] .... come at five o'clock. I finish [6] .... at half past five. But I can come at six o'clock.

B **Listen again and check your answers.**

3 **Practise with another student.**

1. *STUDENT 1:* Can you come to the party?
   STUDENT 2: Yes, I can. / No, I can't.

2. *STUDENT 1:* Can you sing?
   STUDENT 2: Yes, I can. / No, I can't.

WORDS Verbs

4 A Listen, read and repeat.

1 
watch

2 
sing

3 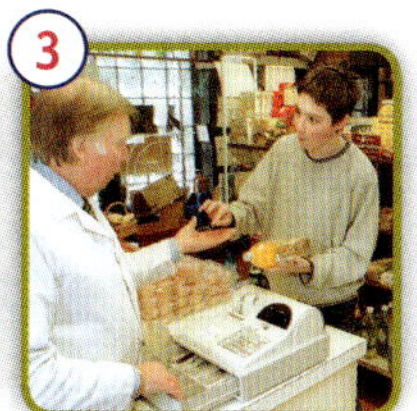
buy

4 
cook

5 
play

6 
dance

7 
write

8 
speak

B What goes with each verb? Choose the correct answer.

1. play the **guitar** / **house**
2. sing a **song** / **dictionary**
3. buy a **book** / **brother**
4. cook **lunch** / **a restaurant**
5. watch **dinner** / **TV**
6. write **an e-mail** / **a party**
7. dance with a **cat** / **friend**
8. speak **Chinese** / **China**

GRAMMAR

5 A Read the grammar box.

Can	
Affirmative	**Negative**
I **can come** to the party. She **can speak** English. — **can** + verb	I **can't come** to the party. She **can't speak** English. — **can't** + verb
Questions	**Short Answers**
Can you **come** to the party? **Can** she **speak** English. — **Can...** + verb...?	Yes, I **can**. / No, I **can't**. Yes, she **can**. / No, she **can't**.

B Complete the sentences with *can* or *can't*.

1. Emily ....can.... speak English.
2. Cats .... read.
3. Children .... buy a car.
4. We're early for the lesson. We .... have a cup of coffee.
5. .... Deshi have dinner with us?
6. Dogs .... cook food.
7. .... you speak Chinese?
8. Henry works at the weekend. He .... come to the party on Saturday.

C Tick (✓) the column which is true for you.

Can you ... ?	Yes, I can.	No, I can't.
1. write a letter in English		
2. play the guitar		
3. cook Chinese food		
4. speak French		
5. dance		

D Tell the class your answers.

WORDS Places in the City

12 A Listen, read and repeat.

bakery cinema hospital club bank clothes shop library post office

B Match the activities to the places.

1

2

ACTIVITY		PLACE
1. buy a cake	....	a. cinema
2. read a book	....	b. clothes shop
3. watch a film	....	c. hospital
4. buy a dress	....	d. bank
5. buy a stamp	....	e. library
6. dance	..1....	f. bakery
7. see a doctor	....	g. post office
8. get money	....	h. club

8

7

3

4

5

6

C **Write sentences about things you do and places you go to, using the words below.**

club cook cinema library watch TV play the guitar bakery dance

1. ....
2. ....
3. ....
4. ....
5. ....
6. ....
7. ....
8. ....

READING

13 **A** **Read about a London department store.**

SELFRIDGES

Selfridges is a very famous department store in London. Every year, millions of people go shopping there. Selfridges is very big and beautiful. It has got eight floors and it sells everything from clothes to computers. You can also buy food from all over the world at Selfridges Food Hall. Selfridges has got many restaurants in the shop as well. On the fifth floor, there is a hair and beauty salon. The average customer spends £51 when he or she visits Selfridges. Today, there are Selfridges stores outside London, so you can go shopping in style in Manchester and in Birmingham, too.

B **Answer the questions.**

1. How many people go shopping at Selfridges every year?

....

2. How many floors has Selfridges got?

....

3. What are three types of things you can buy at Selfridges?

....

4. Where is the hair and beauty salon?

....

5. How much money does the average customer spend at Selfridges?

....

6. Where can you visit Selfridges stores?

....

LANGUAGE PRACTICE pages 96-99

unit 8

I'm doing my homework.

1 **Listen, read and repeat.**

2 **A** **Listen and complete the dialogue.**

EMILY: What's everyone 1........doing........ now, Deshi?

DESHI: I am studying with Danielle. We're doing 2...................... .

EMILY: What 3...................... Henry doing?

DESHI: He's 4...................... a letter to his friend.

EMILY: What about Marisa? 5...................... is she doing, Deshi?

DESHI: She's reading a book.

EMILY: Where's Toni?

DESHI: Toni isn't here.

EMILY: What's he 6...................... ?

DESHI: He's 7...................... his room.

B **Listen again and check your answers.**

3 **Practise with another student.**

STUDENT 1: Are you watching TV?

STUDENT 2: Yes, I am. / No, I'm not.

WORDS Verbs

4 **A Listen, read and repeat.**

1 
sleep

2 
clean

3 
run

4 
go out

5 
play

6 
meet

7 
wait

8 
help

B Match the phrases in columns I and II to make sentences according to the pictures in A.

I		II
1. She is sleeping	......	a. to a club.
2. She is cleaning	......	b. for the train.
3. He is running	......	c. a friend with her homework.
4. They are going out	..1..	d. in her bed.
5. We are playing	......	e. in the park.
6. I am meeting	......	f. games on the computer.
7. He is waiting	......	g. my boyfriend.
8. You are helping	......	h. the car.

GRAMMAR

5 **A Read the grammar box.**

Present Continuous	
Affirmative	
I	**am** working
you / we / they	**are** working
he / she / it	**is** working

B Complete the sentences below using *am*, *is* or *are*.

1. We ......are...... studying French.
2. Cari .... having lunch with Danielle at the moment.
3. Deshi and Toni .... running.
4. Toni .... waiting for me.
5. I .... working in London.
6. You .... reading a good book.
7. The film .... starting now.
8. Shhh! Marisa .... sleeping.

6 A Read the grammar box.

Present Continuous		
Spelling		
wait	>	wai**ting**
live	>	liv**ing**
put	>	put**ting**

B Add *-ing* to the verbs.

1. drive > driving
2. run > ....
3. meet > ....
4. have > ....
5. write > ....
6. get > ....

C Complete the sentences with the verbs in brackets. Use the Present Continuous.

1. Emily ....is teaching.... (teach) her class at the moment.
2. Cari and Marisa .... (sleep) on the sofa.
3. Henry .... (run) in the park.
4. You .... (work) very hard today.
5. I .... (phone) Danielle now.
6. The TV programme .... (start) right now.
7. We .... (watch) TV at the moment.

This match is boring.

7 Listen, read and repeat.

8 A Listen and complete the dialogues.

HENRY: Hi, Marisa. Do you want to go to the 1 ...*cinema*... ?

MARISA: No, sorry. I'm watching the football match right 2 ....

HENRY: Oh, I'm not watching it. It's so boring.

MARISA: Well, Deshi isn't 3 .... the game. Call him.

HENRY: Hi, Deshi. It's very noisy. 4 .... you watching the football match?

DESHI: No, I'm not. I'm 5 .... my room.

HENRY: Hi, Toni. What are you doing?

TONI: I'm 6 .... football with friends.

B Listen again and check your answers.

GRAMMAR

9 A Read the grammar box.

Present Continuous		
Negative		
I **am not** sleeping	>	**'m not** sleeping
he / she / it — is **not** sleeping	>	isn**'t** sleeping
you / we / they — are **not** sleeping	>	aren**'t** sleeping

B Write the sentences in the negative.

1. I am having breakfast at home.
   I am not having breakfast at home.
2. You are listening to me.
   ....
3. My friends are going out now.
   ....
4. Henry is cooking dinner right now.
   ....
5. My parents and I are waiting for you.
   ....
6. The children are playing with their puppy.
   ....

C Imagine it's eight o'clock in the evening. Describe the things your family and friends are doing right now.

It's eight o'clock in the evening. My father is . . .

....

....

....

10 A Read the grammar box.

Present Continuous	
Questions	**Short Answers**
Am I help**ing**?	Yes, I **am**. / No, I**'m not**.
Is he / she / it help**ing**?	Yes, she **is**. / No, she **isn't**.
Are you / we / they help**ing**?	Yes, they **are**. / No, they **aren't**.

B Put the words in the correct order.

1. listening / to music / you / Are / ?
   Are you listening to music?
2. Are / buying / they / the / blue / sofa / ?
   ....
3. Marisa / waiting / Is / for / us / ?
   ....
4. you / Are / English / speaking / ?
   ....
5. Is / singing / Henry / right now / ?
   ....

WORDS Adjectives

11 A Listen, read and repeat.

1 
happy

2 
sad

3 
noisy

4 
quiet

5 
fast

6 
slow

7 
boring

8 
interesting

B Complete the sentences with the words in A.

1. I don't like cleaning my house. It's very ....boring...... for me.
2. People are usually .... when they are sleeping.
3. He runs a kilometre in three minutes. He is a very .... runner.
4. It's sometimes .... in the classroom because we talk to our friends.
5. I like watching football matches. They're always ....
6. Hurry up! Don't be so .... We don't want to be late for school.
7. I'm always .... on my birthday. I have so much fun with my friends.
8. Cari is .... because she can't find her hamster.

PRONUNCIATION

12 **Listen, read and repeat. Pay attention to the pronunciation of the verbs in colour.**

1. The students are studying.
2. Are you talking to me?
3. We are having lunch.
4. I am waiting for you.
5. Is he listening to us?

READING

13 **A** **Read the text about cricket.**

CRICKET

The English love cricket! It is a very old game, but it is very popular today.

It takes a long time to play a cricket game. People can play from the morning until the afternoon. The players often stop for lunch and tea and start playing again. People sometimes play one game for five days!

In cricket, there are two teams. Each team has got 11 players. The teams play on a big pitch. One player throws a ball. A player from the other team hits the ball with his bat. Then he runs very fast. The team with the most "runs" wins the game.

People in other English-speaking countries, for example, Australia, South Africa and New Zealand, play cricket. It is also a very popular sport in India and Pakistan.

B **Tick (✓) the sentences true (T) or false (F).**

	T	F
1. Many people in England love cricket.		
2. Cricket is a new game.		
3. Cricket players can stop the game to have lunch.		
4. There are five players in a team.		
5. One cricket player throws a bat.		
6. The player with the bat hits the ball.		

C **Correct the false sentences in B.**

....

....

....

LANGUAGE PRACTICE pages 100-103

review

WORD LIST

any more	fast	interesting	nothing	run
at the moment	football match	just	on my way	sad
ball	go out	letter	outside	sleep
boring	happen	meet	play	slow
clean	happy	need	quiet	wait
Don't worry	help	noisy	right now	What's wrong?

VOCABULARY

1 **Look at the word list above and do the following exercises.**

1. **List two actions people usually do in their homes.**

   ......clean...... ....

2. **List two actions people do outside their homes.**

   ....

3. **List two pairs of adjectives that are opposites.**

   1. .... – ....
   2. .... – ....

GRAMMAR

2 **Complete the sentences with the verbs in brackets. Use the Present Continuous.**

1. Be quiet. Robert ....is sleeping.... (sleep).
2. I .... (not talk) to you!
3. The children .... (run) to school at the moment.
4. Linda .... (clean) her bedroom right now.
5. We .... (write) an e-mail now.
6. Mike .... (not study).
7. You .... (not listen) to me!
8. My friends and I .... (go out) to a restaurant right now.

3 **Write the sentences as *Yes / No* questions.**

1. You are doing your homework.

   Are you doing your homework?..........

2. Bob is meeting his friends right now.

   ....

3. Kate and Dan are having tea now.

   ....

4. We are listening to music.

   ....

5. I am driving to the cinema at the moment.

   ....

6. You and Mike are watching the football match.

   ....

LISTENING

4 **A Listen and choose the correct answer.**

1. a. Yes, he does. b. No, he isn't.
2. a. We're playing football. b. I get up at five o'clock.
3. a. At a club. b. She's noisy.
4. a. Yes, we can. b. Yes, I am.
5. a. No, it's interesting. b. No, it's sad.

B Listen and check your answers.

LET'S GO: YOUR TURN

1 Listen and read the dialogue.

KATE: Hi, **Sam**. I'm doing my homework and I need your help.

SAM: Sorry, **Kate**, but I **am cleaning my bedroom** right now.

KATE: Oh, is **Dan** there? Can **he** help me?

SAM: No, Dan isn't here. **He**'s **running in the park**. But **Mike** is here. He's doing his homework, too.

2 In pairs, change the words in colour. Act out your new dialogue.

3 Imagine it's nine o'clock in the evening. Ask three students the follwing questions and write their answers.

	Name	What are you doing?	What are your friends doing?
1			
2			
3			

DID YOU KNOW?

The most popular sports in Australia are cricket, swimming and Australian football. In Canada, they like golf and ice hockey. In the United States, they love baseball. Basketball and American football are very popular, too. The British love football, rugby and cricket. Which sports are the most popular in your country?

unit 1 LANGUAGE PRACTICE

Vocabulary Round-Up

Translate the words.

NUMBERS: 0-19

nought / oh	seven	fourteen
one	eight	fifteen
two	nine	sixteen
three	ten	seventeen
four	eleven	eighteen
five	twelve	nineteen
six	thirteen	

COUNTRIES AND NATIONALITIES

Brazil	Nigeria
Brazilian	Nigerian
China	Spain
Chinese	Spanish
England	Turkey
English	Turkish
France	
French	

THE CLASSROOM

board
book
chair
desk
dictionary
notebook
pen
pencil

Translate the useful language.

USEFUL LANGUAGE

Good morning.
Good afternoon.
Good evening.
What's your name?
My name's Emily.
What's your address?
What's your phone number?
How are you?
Fine, thanks.
This is my friend, Danielle.
Nice to meet you.
Where are you from?

Vocabulary Practice

1 **Write the answers in words.**

1. six + four = ...ten......
2. one + seven = ...
3. two + two = ...
4. five - five = ...
5. eight - six = ...
6. four + five = ...
7. seventeen - three = ...
8. nineteen - four = ...
9. thirteen - one = ...
10. eighteen - seven = ...

2 **Do the puzzle. Look at the pictures and find the hidden word.**

					1 n	o	t	e	b	o	o	k
						2						
3												
				4								
						5						
						6						
				7								

The hidden word is ....

3 **Write about the items in the picture.**

1. four desks ....
2. ....
3. ....
4. ....
5. ....
6. ....
7. ....
8. ....

4 **What's the country? Then write the nationality.**

1. aicnh = China ...... - ......Chinese......
2. raingei = N...................... - ....
3. cenraf = F...................... - ....
4. dgalenn = E...................... - ....
5. zirbla = B...................... - ....
6. krtuye = T...................... - ....
7. ipnas = S...................... - ....

Grammar Practice

1 Write the words in the correct place.

~~he~~ we they I it she you

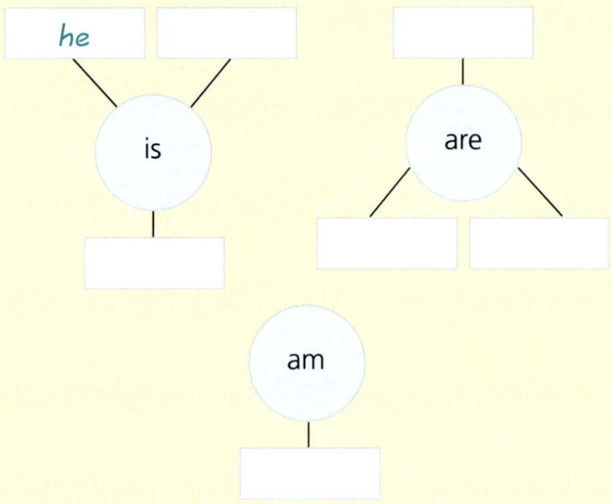

2 Complete the sentences with *am*, *is* or *are*.

1. Where ....*is*.......... he from?
2. Danielle .... from France.
3. I .... from England.
4. .... you from Nigeria?
5. Where .... you from?
6. .... they Chinese?
7. We .... English.
8. It .... 020 8572 9344.

3 Write the contractions.

1. What is this in English?
   What's this in English?........................
2. You are my friend.
   ....
3. It is a desk.
   ....
4. What is your phone number?
   ....
5. I am fine, thanks.
   ....

4 Complete the sentences with *am not*, *is not* or *are not*.

1. It ....*is not*........ a dictionary.
2. I .... a teacher.
3. We .... in Turkey.
4. She .... from Nigeria.
5. You .... my friend.
6. He .... at school.

5 Write the sentences in the negative.

1. I'm from Spain.
   I'm not from Spain...................................
2. She is Turkish.
   ....
3. It is a notebook.
   ....
4. You are Toni.
   ....
5. He is my friend.
   ....
6. They are French.
   ....
7. We are in ESO 2.
   ....

6 Complete the questions with *Am*, *Is* or *Are*.

1. ....*Are*....... you at school?
2. .... your teacher from Spain?
3. .... I at the Albany Hotel?
4. .... Toni your friend?
5. .... the students Turkish?
6. .... your phone number 020 8754 6308?

7 Put the words in the correct order. Then answer the questions.

1. Henry / Nigeria / from / Is / ?
   Is Henry from Nigeria? ....
   ....
2. you / Are / a / student / ?
   ....
   ....
3. Emily / your / name / Is / ?
   ....
   ....
4. your teacher / Is / English / ?
   ....
   ....
5. your friends / Are / Brazilian / ?
   ....
   ....
6. you / at school /Are / ?
   ....
   ....

Language Practice

1 Match the sentences in A to the sentences in B.

A	B
1. Good evening.	...... a. Hello, Marisa!
2. Hi, Emily!	..*1*... b. Good evening.
3. What's your name?	...... c. I'm from Turkey.
4. Where are you from?	...... d. It's 020 8572 9354.
5. What's your phone number?	...... e. My name's Toni.

2 Complete the sentences with the words below.

evening Hi ~~name~~ number Good please

1. What's your ....*name*....... ?
2. ...., I'm Deshi.
3. .... afternoon.
4. What's your phone .... ?
5. What's your address, ... ?
6. Good ...., Danielle.

3 Choose the correct answer.

1. Hi! My name's Alex.
   a. Nice to meet you, Alex. *(circled)*
   b. I'm from London, Alex.
2. How are you?
   a. I'm Alex.
   b. Fine, thanks.
3. What's this?
   a. This is fine.
   b. It's a chair.
4. Are you from London?
   a. Yes, she is.
   b. Yes, I am.

4 Translate the sentences.

1. I am English.
   ....
2. It's a book.
   ....
3. Cari is from Turkey.
   ....
4. I'm fine, thanks.
   ....
5. Good afternoon, students.
   ....
6. What's your address?
   ....

Vocabulary Round-Up

Translate the words.

DAYS OF THE WEEK

Monday
Tuesday
Wednesday
Thursday
Friday
Saturday
Sunday

JOBS

cook
doctor
electrician
housekeeper
porter
receptionist
shop assistant
waiter

NUMBERS: 20-100

twenty	twenty-seven	seventy
twenty-one	twenty-eight	eighty
twenty-two	twenty-nine	ninety
twenty-three	thirty	one hundred
twenty-four	forty	
twenty-five	fifty	
twenty-six	sixty	

Translate the useful language.

USEFUL LANGUAGE

What's your job?
My boyfriend is a receptionist, too.
Is she a receptionist?
No, she isn't. She's a cook.
How old are you?
I'm eighteen years old.
What's your address?
It's 34 Brook Road.
What's this?
Are those Spanish books?

Vocabulary Practice

1 **Complete the jobs with *a, e, i, o* or *u*. Then match the jobs to the pictures.**

..d.. 1. w..a..i..t..e..r

...... 2. d ... c t ... r

...... 3. h ...... s ... k ...... p ... r

...... 4. r ... c ... p t ...... n ... s t

...... 5. ... l ... c t r ... c ...... n

...... 6. c ...... k

...... 7. p ... r t ... r

...... 8. s h ... p ... s s ... s t ... n t

a

b

c

d

e

f

g

h

2 **Write the answers in words.**

1. 7 x 10 = ...seventy.....
2. 6 x 6 = ...
3. 100 - 5 = ...
4. 5 x 8 = ...
5. 30 + 20 = ...
6. 2 x 40 = ...
7. 100 - 75 = ...
8. 100 - 22 = ...
9. 6 x 7 = ...
10. 9 x 9 = ...

3 **Find the days of the week in the puzzle. Then write them in the correct order.**

w	s	a	t	u	r	d	a	y
x	e	r	m	q	t	v	x	e
z	d	d	o	a	h	l	t	t
f	i	o	n	r	u	k	y	u
g	j	l	d	e	r	m	s	e
n	m	p	a	d	s	n	j	s
y	s	w	y	b	d	d	i	d
z	s	u	n	d	a	y	a	a
f	r	i	d	a	y	p	h	y

1. Monday..
2. ....
3. ....
4. ....
5. ....
6. ....
7. ....

Grammar Practice

1 Match the pronouns in A to the possessive adjectives in B.

A		B
1. he	......	a. their
2. she	......	b. its
3. it	......	c. my
4. we	......	d. your
5. they	..1..	e. his
6. I	......	f. her
7. you	......	g. our

2 Complete the sentences with the correct possessive adjective.

1. Hi! ......My...... name is Danielle.
2. What's .... job? Are you a receptionist?
3. Look! That's Danielle and .... boyfriend, Paul.
4. That's Henry and that's .... teacher, Emily.
5. I'm Marisa. What's .... name?
6. We are students. This is .... school.
7. They are at the hotel. .... friends are at the hotel, too.

3 Complete the chart with the words below.

~~pencil~~ notebook ambulance hotel electrician address desk English book

A	An
pencil	

4 Complete the sentences with *a* or *an*.

1. Emily is ......an...... English teacher.
2. Marisa is .... cook at the hotel.
3. David is .... electrician.
4. Her boyfriend is .... doctor.
5. Henry is .... waiter.
6. It's .... French restaurant.

5 Complete the chart.

Singular	Plural
telephone	telephones
dictionary	
pen	
cook	
teacher	

6 Complete the sentences with *this, that, these* or *those*.

1. ......This...... is my friend.

2. Look! .... is my friend.

3. Excuse me, what's .... in English?

4. Jane, ... are my parents.

5. Look! .... are my friends.

6. Where are .... books from?

7 Write the sentences in the plural.

1. He is a waiter.
   They are waiters.
2. This is a French dictionary.
   ....
3. I am from England.
   ....
4. Is she a student?
   ....
5. That is a chair.
   ....
6. I am not a doctor.
   ....

Language Practice

1 Match the questions in A to their answers in B.

A

1. What's your address?
2. How old are you?
3. Are you a shop assistant?
4. What's her job?
5. How old is David?

B

...... a. He's 15 years old.
..1... b. It's 44 Pimlico Road.
...... c. No, I'm not. I'm a receptionist.
...... d. I'm 18 years old.
...... e. She's an English teacher.

2 Complete the sentences with the words below.

waiter job ~~old~~ those Her

1. How ....old.... are you? Are you seventeen?
2. He is a .... at a Chinese restaurant.
3. Cari is a receptionist. .... boyfriend is a receptionist, too.
4. What's your ....? Are you a doctor?
5. Are .... Spanish books?

3 Choose the correct answer.

1. What's your job?
   a. I'm English.
   (b.) I'm a receptionist.
2. How old are you?
   a. I'm seventeen years old.
   b. I'm Spanish.
3. Is she a cook?
   a. No, she isn't. She's a doctor.
   b. No, she isn't. She's eighteen years old.
4. What's your address?
   a. It's Monday.
   b. It's 67 Green Road.
5. What's your father's job?
   a. He's an electrician.
   b. She's an electrician.

4 Translate the sentences.

1. What's this?
   ....
2. How old are you?
   ....
3. What's your job?
   ....
4. Are you a doctor?
   ....
5. She is a housekeeper.
   ....

Vocabulary Round-Up

Translate the words.

THE FAMILY

aunt	grandmother
brother	grandparents
child	husband
children	mother
daughter	parents
father	sister
grandchild	son
grandchildren	uncle
grandfather	wife

COLOURS

black	pink
blue	purple
brown ;	red
green	white
grey	yellow
orange	

PARTS OF THE BODY

arm	hand
body	head
ear	leg
eye	mouth
finger	nose
foot	toe
hair	

Translate the useful language.

USEFUL LANGUAGE

Are you married?

Have you got any brothers or sisters?

Have you got a boyfriend?

What's new?

Has she got brown eyes?

What colour are his eyes?

He's got blue eyes.

I've got some photos.

Vocabulary Practice

1 Match the words in A to their pairs in B.

A		B
1. mother	......	a. son
2. brother	......	b. wife
3. husband	......	c. sister
4. grandmother	......	d. aunt
5. uncle	..1...	e. father
6. daughter	......	f. grandfather

2 Complete Simon's family tree with the words in Exercise 1.

3 Complete the colours with *a*, *e*, *i*, *o* or *u*.

1. y .e. ll .o. w
2. bl ......
3. gr ...... n
4. br ... wn
5. p ... rpl ...
6. ... r ... ng ...
7. wh ... t ...
8. bl ... ck

4 Write the words in the correct places.

hair ~~eye~~ nose mouth
ear arm hand finger
leg foot

1. ....eye.........
2. ....
3. ....
4. ....
5. ....
6. ....
7. ....
8. ....
9. ....
10. ....

Grammar Practice

1 Complete the sentences with *have got* or *has got*.

1. The students ....have got.... books.
2. We .... three children.
3. She .... a brother.
4. You .... brown eyes.
5. Toni .... three uncles.
6. I .... a sister.

2 Write the sentences in the negative.

1. Susan has got two sisters.
   Susan hasn't got two sisters.
2. Paul has got grandchildren.
   ....
3. We have got 15 students in our class.
   ....
4. You have got blue eyes.
   ....
5. I have got my mother's nose.
   ....
6. The dog has got black ears.
   ....

3 Complete the questions with *Have ... got* or *Has ... got*.

1. ....Has....... she ......got........ your phone number?
2. .... you .... a brother?
3. .... I .... your dictionary?
4. .... he .... a girlfriend?
5. .... they .... blue eyes?

4 Put the words in the correct order.

1. you / Have / got / boyfriend / a / ?
   Have you got a boyfriend?
2. got / eyes / green / They've / .
   ....
3. any / children / haven't / I / got / .
   ....
4. sisters / Have / got / any / you / ?
   ....
5. got / hasn't / blue / She / eyes / .
   ....
6. got / Tom / brother / has / a / .
   ....

5 Write the words in the correct place.

~~aunt~~ coffee house money electrician time flat book ambulance

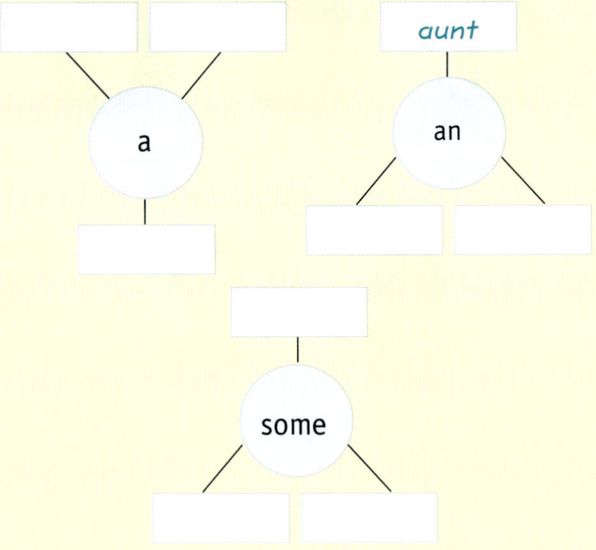

6 Choose the correct answer.

1. We've got **some** / **any** water.
2. Have you got **some** / **any** brothers?
3. I haven't got **some** / **any** homework today.
4. Look at **some** / **any** photos.
5. They haven't got **some** / **any** money.

7 Look at the picture. Complete the sentences. Use the Saxon Genitive.

1. Simon is ....Mary's.... husband.
2. Ruth and James are Mary and .... children.
3. Ruth is .... sister.
4. James is .... brother.
5. Mary is .... wife.
6. Simon and Mary are James and .... parents.

Language Practice

1 Match the questions in A to their answers in B.

A

1. Has she got a boyfriend?
2. Have they got any brothers or sisters?
3. What colour is his hair?
4. What colour are her eyes?
5. Are you married?
6. Is she married?

B

...... a. No, she isn't.
...... b. Yes, I am.
...... c. It's brown.
...... d. Yes, they've got a sister.
..1... e. Yes, she has.
...... f. They're blue.

2 Complete the sentences with the words below.

eyes photos married new ~~sisters~~

1. Have you got any brothers or ....sisters.... ?
2. What colour are his .... ?
3. Are you .... ?
4. I've got some ....
5. What's .... ?

3 Choose the correct answer.

1. Have you got any brothers or sisters?
   a. I've got three children.
   (b.) No, I haven't.
2. Are you married?
   a. Yes, I am.
   b. No, I haven't.
3. What colour are your eyes?
   a. It's blue.
   b. They're blue.
4. Has she got blue eyes?
   a. Yes, she has.
   b. No, she likes purple.
5. Have you got a girlfriend?
   a. Yes, I have.
   b. No, she isn't.

4 Translate the sentences.

1. Are you married?

   ....

2. Have they got any brothers?

   ....

3. I haven't got any sisters.

   ....

4. I've got a boyfriend.

   ....

5. What colour is your hair?

   ....

unit 4 LANGUAGE PRACTICE

Vocabulary Round-Up

Translate the words.

ADJECTIVES

beautiful
big
blond(e)
dark
fat
good-looking
long
middle-aged
old
short ;
small
tall
thin
ugly
young

PETS

cat
dog
fish
hamster
kitten
puppy
rabbit
snake

Translate the useful language.

USEFUL LANGUAGE

She's beautiful.
Here's a photo of Daniel.
She's got blonde hair.
He's tall and thin.
Are you tall?
Have you got long hair?
Excuse me.
How many puppies are there?
I know.
Have you got any snakes?
How much is this snake?

Vocabulary Practice

1 Match the adjectives in A to their opposites in B.

A		B
1. tall	......	a. ugly
2. beautiful	......	b. small
3. young	......	c. fat
4. big	..1..	d. short
5. blonde	......	e. old
6. thin	......	f. dark

2 Label the pictures with the words in Exercise 1.

1. ....ugly.... 2. ....

3. .... 4. ....

5. .... 6. ....

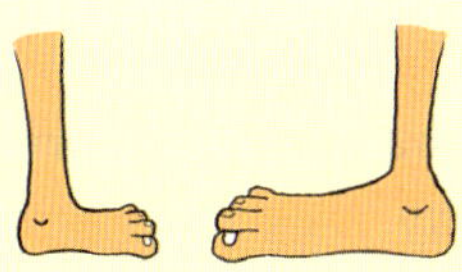

7. .... 8. ....

9. .... 10. ....

11. .... 12. ....

3 Find eight animals in the puzzle and list them.

h	r	a	b	b	i	t
s	a	k	p	y	d	o
n	o	m	a	t	o	n
a	f	i	s	h	g	y
k	c	c	a	t	k	h
e	k	i	t	t	e	n
u	p	u	p	p	y	r

1. ....rabbit.... 5. ....
2. .... 6. ....
3. .... 7. ....
4. .... 8. ....

4 Complete the sentences with the words below.

kittens blonde snakes puppies
~~middle-aged~~ tall old small

1. Dan isn't young and he isn't old. He's .middle-aged. .
2. How many .... has your cat got?
3. Kate's hair isn't dark. It's ....
4. Hamsters are .... animals.
5. Sharon isn't short. She's very ....
6. .... haven't got any arms or legs.
7. My dog has got six ....
8. Our cat is .... He's twelve.

LANGUAGE PRACTICE

Vocabulary Round-Up

Translate the words.

ROOMS OF THE HOUSE

bathroom	garden
bedroom	kitchen
dining room	living room
garage	toilet

FURNITURE

bed	lamp
bookshelves	poster
cooker	rug
cupboard	sofa
fridge	table

ORDINAL NUMBERS: 1ST-12TH

first	seventh
second	eighth
third	ninth
fourth	tenth
fifth	eleventh
sixth	twelfth

Translate the useful language.

USEFUL LANGUAGE

Where do you live in Brazil?
I live in a small flat.
Do you like your flat?
My bedroom is very big.
It's very nice.
The colours are ugly.
Have you got any posters of animals?
Here they are.
What about this poster?
Let's go to the second floor.
You like going shopping.

Vocabulary Practice

1 **Complete the places around the house with *a, e, i, o* or *u*.**

1. b .e. dr .o. .o. m
2. b ... thr ...... m
3. k ... tch ... n
4. l ... v ... ng r ...... m
5. d ... n ... ng r ...... m
6. g ... r ... g ...
7. t ...... l ... t
8. g ... rd ... n

2 **Match the ordinal numbers to the cardinal numbers. Then write the ordinal numbers in the correct order.**

CARDINAL		ORDINAL
1. three	......	a. tenth
2. seven	......	b. eighth
3. six	......	c. second
4. eight	......	d. ninth
5. four	..1...	e. third
6. nine	......	f. fourth
7. eleven	......	g. sixth
8. two	......	h. first
9. twelve	......	i. fifth
10. one	......	j. seventh
11. five	......	k. twelfth
12. ten	......	l. eleventh

1. ......first......	7. ....
2.	8. ....
3.	9. ....
4.	10. ....
5.	11. ....
6.	12. ....

3 **Look at the pictures and complete the puzzle.**

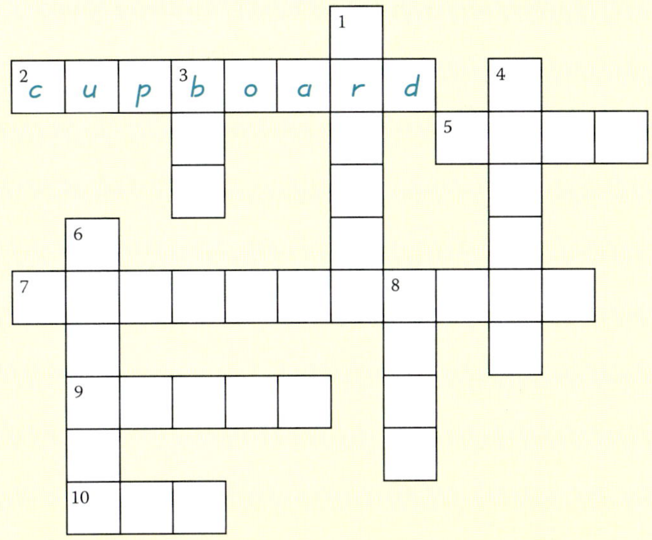

ACROSS ▶

2
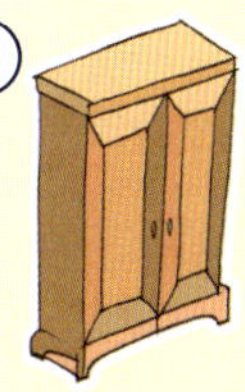
5

7

9

10
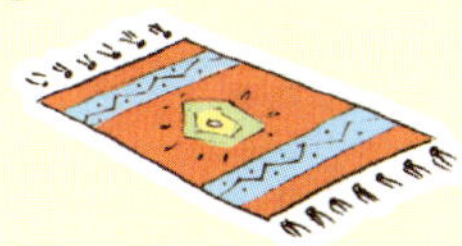

DOWN ▼

1

3
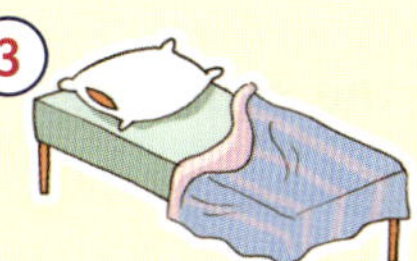
4

6

8
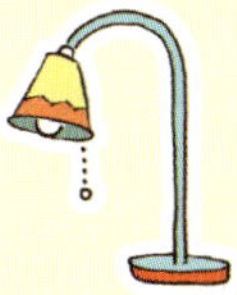

Grammar Practice

1 **Complete the sentences with *live / lives, like / likes* or *work / works*.**

1. They ....live.... in a big house.
2. Brad .... in a small restaurant.
3. I .... your bedroom. It's beautiful!
4. Danielle .... in a flat.
5. We .... this rug.
6. Emily .... at the hotel.

2 **Complete the chart.**

I / you / we / they	he / she / it
1. like	likes
2. read	
3. do	
4. dance	
5. watch	
6. get	
7. finish	
8. love	
9. go	
10. study	
11. teach	
12. live	

3 **Complete the sentences.**

1. I study English at school.
   He studies English at school.
2. You live in Turkey.
   She ....
3. We work on Saturdays.
   He ....
4. Dogs like children.
   It ....
5. They teach at the hotel.
   She ....

4 **Complete the sentences with the correct form of the verbs below.**

study go work teach ~~like~~ read

1. Emily ....likes.... Turkish food.
2. Cari .... English at the hotel.
3. Luke and Janice .... at a restaurant. They are waiters.
4. Marisa .... to a computer class on Mondays.
5. Emily .... English at the hotel.
6. I .... books in Chinese in the evenings.

5 **Match A to B to make sentences.**

A		B
1. Tom likes	......	a. French at school.
2. We work	......	b. her homework at the weekend.
3. They go	......	c. at the hotel.
4. She studies	......	d. to a big school.
5. Carol does	..1..	e. that poster.

6 **Complete the sentences with the words below.**

Italian food living going ~~likes~~ listening

1. Henry ....likes.... his job.
2. I like ....
3. Marisa likes .... to shops.
4. We like .... to jazz music.
5. Alberto likes .... in Seville.

7 **Put the words in the correct order.**

1. likes / Helen / the hotel / at / working
   Helen likes working at the hotel.
2. I / Tuesdays / like
   ....
3. a flat / like / We / in / living
   ....
4. likes / poster / this / Mark
   ....
5. like / studying / You / English
   ....
6. dogs / like / They
   ....

Language Practice

1 **Match the questions in A to their answers in B.**

A		B
1. Do you like this table?	......	a. Yes, we have. Here they are.
2. Have you got any rugs?	......	b. They're on the first floor.
3. Where do you live?	..1...	c. Yes, I do.
4. Where are the sofas?	......	d. No, they're ugly.
5. Do you like the colours?	......	e. In a small house.

2 **Complete the sentences with the words below.**

small Let's ugly ~~live~~ like

1. Where do you .....live..... ?
2. .... go to the third floor.
3. The colours are ....
4. I live in a .... flat.
5. Do you .... this rug?

3 **Choose the correct answer.**

1. Where do you live?
   (a.) I live in a small flat.
   b. I like London.
2. Have you got a garden?
   a. It's in the living room.
   b. Yes, I have.
3. Where's Ann?
   a. It's on the sixth floor.
   b. She's in the kitchen.
4. Do you like this lamp?
   a. Yes, it's nice.
   b. It's blue.
5. Where are the fridges?
   a. They're ugly.
   b. They're on the second floor.

4 **Translate the sentences.**

1. I like reading books in the garden.
   ....
2. Where is the toilet?
   ....
3. We live in a small flat.
   ....
4. Let's go to the fifth floor.
   ....
5. Have you got a dining room?
   ....
6. I like your rug.
   ....

Vocabulary Round-Up

Translate the words.

THE TIME

It's (five) o'clock.
It's half past (five).
It's midday.
It's midnight.
It's quarter past (five).
It's quarter to (five).
It's ten past (five).
It's ten to (five).

DAILY ROUTINES

finish school
get home
get up
go to bed
start school

MEALS

have breakfast
have dinner
have lunch
have tea

Translate the useful language.

USEFUL LANGUAGE

What's wrong with Deshi?
He always goes to bed late.
I'm often tired in the morning.
Why are you tired?
I'm sorry I'm late.
Are you OK?
Do you start school early?
What's the time?
Let's have dinner at a restaurant this evening.
That's a great idea.
Do you like Chinese food?
When do you have breakfast?

Vocabulary Practice

1 Write the times in numbers.

1. quarter past eight ....8.15........
2. midnight ....
3. quarter to two ....
4. four o'clock ....
5. ten to seven ....
6. half past nine ....
7. quarter to six ....
8. midday ....
9. ten past ten ....
10. eleven o'clock ....

2 Write the times in words.

1. 6.15 ....quarter past six............
2. 7.45 ....
3. 9.30 ....
4. 10.00 ....
5. 11.15 ....
6. 1.10 ....
7. 3.30 ....
8. 5.50 ....

3 Complete the chart with the words below.

~~three o'clock~~ breakfast
half past twelve finish school
go to bed tea quarter to nine
dinner get home

The Time	Daily Routines	Meals
three o'clock		

4 Look at the pictures. Complete the sentences about Chris with the words below.

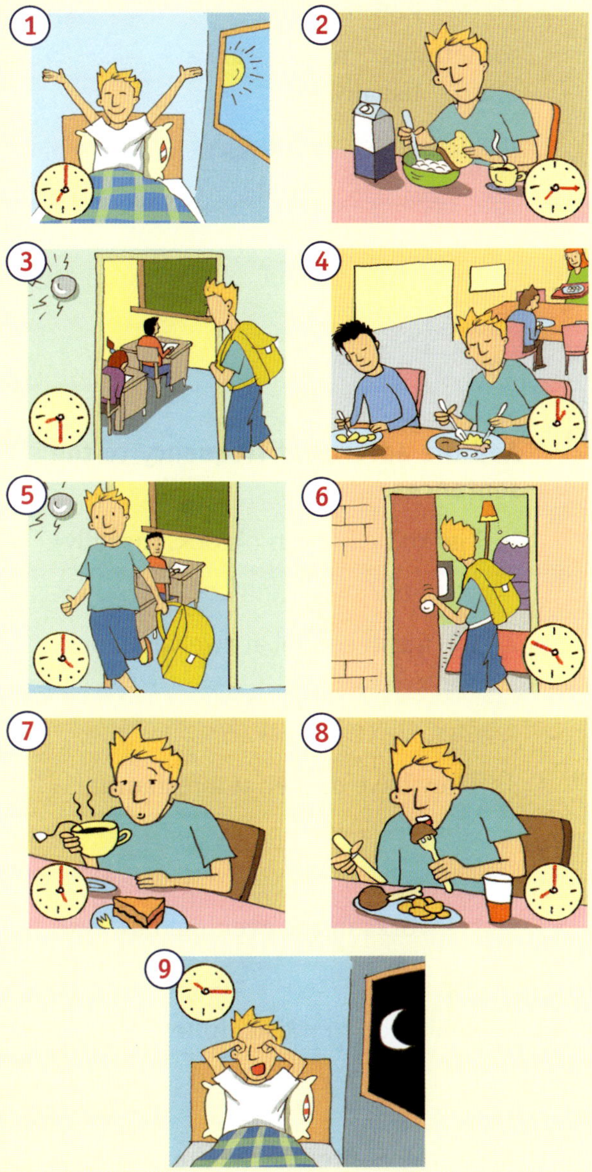

go to bed have lunch start school
have breakfast ~~get up~~ have dinner
get home have tea finish school

1. I ......get up........ at seven o'clock.
2. I .... at quarter past seven.
3. I .... at half past eight.
4. I .... at one o'clock.
5. I .... at four o'clock.
6. I .... at ten to five.
7. I .... at five o'clock.
8. I .... at eight o'clock.
9. I .... at quarter past ten.

Grammar Practice

1 **Write the adverbs of frequency in the correct places.**

sometimes never ~~always~~
often usually

100%
1. always
2. ....
3. ....
4. ....
5. ....

0%

2 **Add the adverbs of frequency to the sentences.**

1. I go to bed at ten o'clock. (usually)
   I usually go to bed at ten o'clock.
2. We finish school at twelve o'clock. (never)
   ....
3. They have dinner at a restaurant. (sometimes)
   ....
4. He works in the evening. (always)
   ....
5. You listen to music. (often)
   ....

3 **Write the sentences in the negative.**

1. He gets up early.
   He doesn't get up early.
2. I start work in the morning.
   ....
3. Danielle and Toni go out in the evening.
   ....
4. Emily reads in the evening.
   ....
5. My friends live in London.
   ....
6. Toni gets up very late.
   ....

4 **Complete the sentences with the verbs in brackets. Use the Present Simple negative.**

1. I don't study (study) French.
2. We .... (watch) TV in the evening.
3. He .... (do) his homework at night.
4. The students .... (go) to the restaurant every day.
5. Sue .... (read) Turkish books.
6. The cat .... (have) dinner in the kitchen.

5 **Complete the questions with *do* or *does*.**

1. Does Toni work in the morning?
2. .... your parents live in London?
3. .... you get up early?
4. When .... your teacher start work?
5. .... Marisa usually have breakfast?
6. When .... school finish?

6 **Match the answers to the questions in Exercise 5.**

...... a. No, she doesn't.
...... b. At nine o'clock.
...... c. No, they don't.
...... d. At half past three.
..1... e. Yes, he does.
...... f. Yes, I do.

7 Write the sentences as *Yes* / *No* questions.

1. He listens to the radio.
   Does he listen to the radio?
2. Henry works in a restaurant.
   ....
3. Danielle and Toni have dinner at eight.
   ....
4. Emily teaches English.
   ....
5. Cari studies English.
   ....
6. You have tea at midnight.
   ....
7. The students go to school at half past seven.
   ....
8. The lesson starts at quarter to ten.
   ....

Language Practice

1 Match the questions in A to their answers in B.

A

1. Are you OK?
2. Do you like Chinese food?
3. Does your mother start work early?
4. Why are you tired?
5. When do you have lunch?

B

...... a. Yes, I do.
...... b. Because I finish work late.
..1... c. Yes, I am.
...... d. At half past one.
...... e. No, she doesn't.

2 Complete the sentences with the words below.

quarter tonight finish Fridays ~~late~~

1. I'm tired because I go to bed ....late........ .
2. I usually .... work at midnight.
3. It's .... past four.
4. Let's have dinner at a restaurant ....
5. I don't work on ....

3 Choose the correct answer.

1. When do you have dinner?
   (a.) At eight o'clock.
   b. It's eight o'clock.
2. Do you like French food?
   a. Yes, I am.
   b. Yes, I do.
3. Do you get up early?
   a. No, I don't.
   b. At half past seven.
4. What's the time?
   a. At quarter past eleven.
   b. It's quarter past eleven.
5. Is Alex OK?
   a. Yes, he is.
   b. No, I don't.

4 Translate the sentences.

1. I finish work at eleven o'clock.
   ....
2. She always goes to bed very late.
   ....
3. What's the time?
   ....
4. It's half past six.
   ....
5. When do you usually have breakfast?
   ....

unit 7

LANGUAGE PRACTICE

Vocabulary Round-Up

Translate the words.

VERBS

buy	sing
cook	speak
dance	watch
play	write

MONTHS OF THE YEAR

January	July
February	August
March	September
April	October
May	November
June	December

PLACES IN THE CITY

- bakery
- bank
- cinema
- clothes shop
- club
- hospital
- library
- post office

Translate the useful language.

USEFUL LANGUAGE

Let's start a rock group.

I can write songs.

Who is that?

What's wrong?

Can you sing?

Don't worry.

Can you come to the party?

When's your birthday?

My birthday's in August.

Let's go to the cinema.

Great idea!

Is Saturday good?

Yes, of course.

Vocabulary Practice

1 Complete the verbs with *a, e, i, o* or *u*. Then match the verbs to the pictures.

..e.. 1. w .a. tch	...... 5. dr ... v ...
...... 2. s ... ng	...... 6. d ... nc ...
...... 3. b ... y	...... 7. wr ... t ...
...... 4. c ...... k	...... 8. sp ...... k

2 Put the months of the year and the days of the week in the correct chart. Write them in the correct order.

October August February Tuesday ~~January~~ December March Thursday July April ~~Monday~~ May Friday September Sunday Wednesday June Saturday November

Months of the Year	
January	

Days of the Week	
Monday	

3 Find eight places in the city in the puzzle and write them under the correct picture.

c	l	o	t	h	e	s	s	h	o	p
i	b	c	p	o	s	l	b	t	f	o
n	f	l	a	s	f	e	n	a	p	b
e	s	u	o	p	e	f	o	k	n	a
m	a	b	l	i	b	r	a	r	y	k
a	p	o	s	t	o	f	f	i	c	e
b	i	t	b	a	k	e	r	y	h	y
m	p	e	m	l	i	b	p	o	t	s

1. clothes shop

2. ....

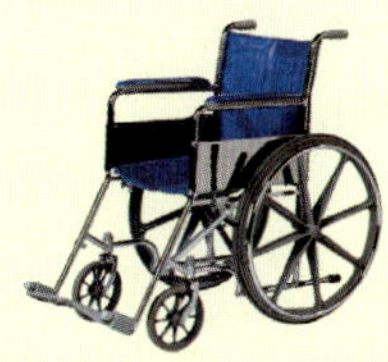
3. ....

4. ....

5. ....

6. ....

7. ....

8. ....

Grammar Practice

1 Complete the sentences with *can* or *can't*.

1. Tom ....can.......... play the guitar. He's very good at it.
2. Rachel .... come to the party on Saturday. She works on Saturday.
3. We .... buy the dog. We haven't got any money.
4. I .... cook dinner. I'm a great cook.
5. You .... speak to the teacher. She isn't here.

2 Use the words below to write sentences that are true for you.

I → can / can't → drive / cook / speak / sing / write → Chinese food / opera / an e-mail / a car / Spanish

1. ....
2. ....
3. ....
4. ....
5. ....

3 Answer the questions to make them true for you.

1. Can you speak Japanese?

   ....
2. Can your father cook dinner?

   ....
3. Can your friends dance?

   ....
4. Can you write a book?

   ....

4 Put the words in the correct order. Then look at the pictures and answer the questions.

1. Lisa / Can / talk / ?

   Can Lisa talk?..

   No, she can't...
2. English / read / Chang / Can / ?

   ....

   ....
3. Megan / the car / drive / Can / ?

   ....

   ....
4. dance / the boys / Can / ?

   ....

   ....
5. Sarah and Adam / Can /cook / ?

   ....

   ....

1
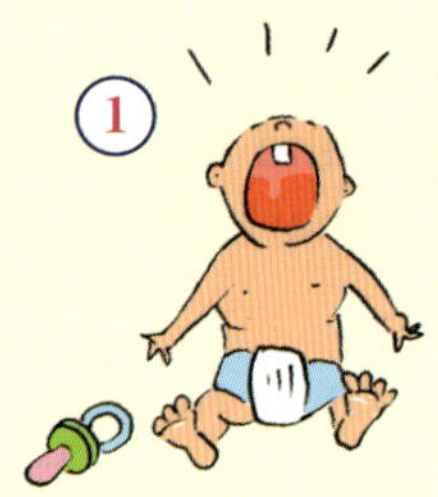
2

3

4

5

5 Complete the chart.

~~the weekend~~ January half past three
Friday Sunday afternoon the evening
May night Wednesday

In	On	At
		the weekend

6 **Choose the correct answer.**

1. Peter's birthday party is on **March** / **Wednesday**.
2. Our holiday is in **Friday** / **June**.
3. The English test is on **Monday morning** / **April**.
4. My computer class is in the **afternoon** / **Sunday**.
5. Anne's birthday is in **Tuesday** / **September**.
6. My English lesson is on **July** / **Thursday afternoon**.
7. I do my homework at **the weekend** / **Sunday**.
8. The lesson starts at **the morning** / **half past nine**.

Language Practice

1 **Match the questions in A to their answers in B.**

A		B
1. Who is that?	......	a. I'm tired.
2. When's your birthday?	..1...	b. It's Tom.
3. What's wrong?	......	c. No, she can't.
4. Can you sing?	......	d. Yes, I can.
5. Can Rachel come to the party?	......	e. No, I finish work at five o'clock.
6. Is four o'clock OK?	......	f. It's in March.

2 **Complete the sentences with the words below.**

worry dance go ~~birthday's~~
start party that write

1. My ..birthday's...in July.
2. Don't ....
3. Can you come to the .... ?
4. Let's .... to the cinema.
5. I can .... songs.
6. Let's .... a rock group.
7. Can you .... ?
8. Who is .... ?

3 **Choose the correct answer.**

1. Let's start a rock group.
   a. Great idea!
   b. Yes, we can.
2. Can you come to the party?
   a. I'm late.
   b. No, I can't.
3. Can you cook English food?
   a. I like it.
   b. Yes, I can.
4. When's your birthday?
   a. It's in December.
   b. It's at five o'clock.
5. Let's go to the cinema.
   a. No, let's go to hospital.
   b. No, let's go to a restaurant.

4 **Translate the sentences.**

1. We can speak English.

   ....

2. I can't come to the party.

   ....

3. My birthday's in August.

   ....

4. I can buy a birthday cake.

   ....

5. Let's have a party on Sunday.

   ....

Vocabulary Round-Up

Translate the words.

VERBS

clean
go out
help
meet ;
play
run
sleep
wait

ADJECTIVES

boring
fast
happy
interesting
noisy
quiet
sad
slow

Translate the useful language.

USEFUL LANGUAGE

I need your help.
I don't know how to do my homework.
Are you watching TV?
What's everyone doing?
Toni isn't here.
I'm on my way.
This match is boring.
Be quiet!
Do you want to go to the cinema?

Vocabulary Practice

1 **What's the verb? Write the verbs. Then match them to the pictures.**

..f... 1. tiaw ......wait......
...... 2. pleh ....
...... 3. yalp ....
...... 4. teem ....
...... 5. og tuo ....
...... 6. nclae ....
...... 7. nru ....
...... 8. plees ....

a

b

c

d

e
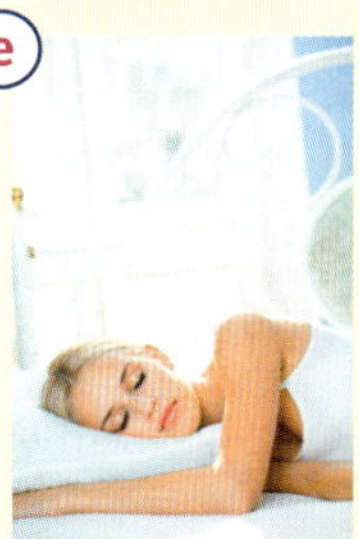
f

g

h

2 **Write the words as pairs of opposites.**

~~happy~~ noisy boring slow
interesting ~~sad~~ quiet fast

......happy...... ......sad......
....
....
....

3 **Complete the puzzle. Look at the clues below.**

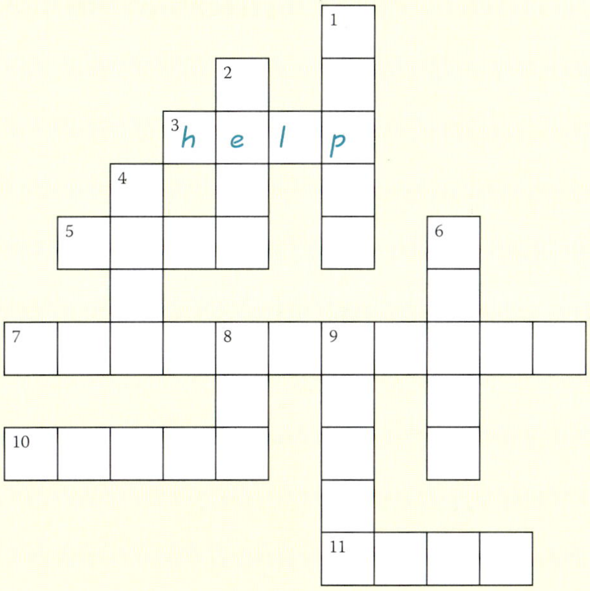

ACROSS ▶

3. I can't do my homework. Please .... me.
5. Let's .... for the bus.
7. The opposite of *boring* is ....
10. Please .... your room.
11. Can you .... the guitar?

DOWN ▼

1. The opposite of *sad* is ....
2. I sometimes .... my friends at the library.
4. The opposite of *slow* is ....
6. The opposite of *noisy* is ....
8. I can .... fast.
9. I'm tired. I want to ....

Grammar Practice

1 Complete the sentences with *am*, *is* or *are*.

1. Henry and Deshi ....*are*.... eating right now.
2. Danielle .... waiting for me at school.
3. I .... working right now.
4. You .... talking to me.
5. Marisa .... reading a book at the moment.
6. We .... listening to music.

2 Complete the chart.

1.	dance	*dancing*
2.	play	
3.	sleep	
4.	do	
5.	study	
6.	live	
7.	run	
8.	write	
9.	get	
10.	teach	
11.	wait	
12.	talk	

3 Complete the sentences with the verbs in brackets. Use the Present Continuous affirmative.

1. Toni and you ...*are writing*... (write) an e-mail.
2. I .... (watch) TV right now.
3. The dog .... (eat) now.
4. Cari .... (clean) the flat at the moment.
5. We .... (study) for an English test.
6. Deshi .... (drive) to work right now.

4 Write the sentences in Exercise 3 in the negative.

1. *Toni and you aren't writing an e-mail.*
2. ....
3. ....
4. ....
5. ....
6. ....

5 Write the sentences as *Yes / No* questions.

1. You are listening to me.
   Are you listening to me?
2. Emily is teaching at the moment.
   ....
3. We are dancing now.
   ....
4. Deshi and Cari are talking right now.
   ....
5. I am helping you.
   ....

6 Complete the questions with the verbs in brackets. Use the Present Continuous. Then complete the answers.

1. ....*Are*.... they ....*playing*.... (play) in the park now?
   No, ..*they aren't*.. .
2. .... I .... (talk) to Ben?
   No, ...
3. .... Emily .... (teach) at the moment?
   No, ...
4. .... Michael and Debbie .... (dance) right now?
   Yes, ...
5. .... you .... (listen) to this song?
   Yes, ...

7 Put the words in the correct order.

1. is / Mark / at the moment / a book / reading / .
   Mark is reading a book at the moment.
2. doing / my homework / am not / right now / I / .
   ....
3. you / listening / to me / Are / ?
   ....
4. going / We / to school / now / aren't / .
   ....
5. waiting / for you / Hazel / Is / ?
   ....
6. The students / right now / are / studying / .
   ....
7. isn't / Luke / right now / in the park / running / .
   ....
8. I / your lunch / eating / Am / ?
   ....

Language Practice

1 Match the questions in A to their answers in B.

A

1. Do you want to watch the football match?
2. Are you cleaning your room?
3. Where's Linda?
4. What's everyone doing?
5. What's wrong?

B

...... a. She isn't here.
...... b. I don't know how to do my homework.
...... c. No, I'm not.
...... d. We're having lunch.
..1... e. No, I don't.

2 Complete the sentences with the words below.

on ~~need~~ quiet boring everyone

1. I ......need....... your help.
2. I'm .... my way.
3. This match is ....
4. What's .... doing?
5. Be .... !

3 Choose the correct answer.

1. Are you working now?
   (a.) Yes, I am.
   b. Yes, I do.
2. Do you want to go to the cinema?
   a. No, I don't.
   b. No, I'm not.
3. What's Brian doing?
   a. He's fine.
   b. He's cleaning his room.
4. Be quiet! Janice is sleeping.
   a. She's on her way.
   b. She's not sleeping any more.
5. What are you doing?
   a. I'm watching TV.
   b. I need your help.

4 Translate the sentences.

1. I'm on my way.
   ....
2. This match is boring.
   ....
3. What's everyone doing?
   ....
4. I'm not sleeping any more.
   ....

GRAMMAR EXTENSION

Past Simple: *To be*

1 **Read the grammar box.**

Affirmative		Negative		Questions		
I / he / she / it	**was**	I / he / she / it	**was not (wasn't)**	**Was**	I / he / she / it	... ?
we / you / they	**were**	we / you / they	**were not (weren't)**	**Were**	we / you / they	... ?

Short Answers: Yes, I **was**. / No, I **wasn't**. Yes, you **were**. / No, you **weren't**.

2 **Complete the sentences with *was* or *were*.**

1. I ....was.... at school yesterday.
2. The boys .... in the classroom at eight o'clock.
3. Sunday .... a good day.
4. Janice and Mark .... late last night.
5. My teacher .... sad last week.

3 **Write the sentences in Exercise 2 in the negative.**

1. I wasn't at school yesterday.
2. ....
3. ....
4. ....
5. ....

4 **Complete the sentences with the affirmative or negative past form of the verb *to be*.**

1. Helen ....wasn't.... (not) at the party last night.
2. The students .... at the library yesterday.
3. We .... (not) happy about the test last week.
4. Lisa and Chris .... twelve years old last year.
5. Gary .... (not) my friend two years ago.

5 **Complete the questions with *Was* or *Were*.**

1. ....Were.... you on television last week?
2. .... the party on Friday?
3. .... Mike and Alan in your class last year?
4. .... the books on your desk ten minutes ago?
5. .... Rachel in England in September?

6 **Complete the answers to the questions in Exercise 5.**

1. Yes, I was .
2. No, ...
3. No, ...
4. Yes, ...
5. No, ...

Past Simple: Affirmative

1 Read the grammar box.

Affirmative	Spelling Rules
I you he she it we you they — walk**ed**	regular: walk – walk**ed** but: danc**e** – danc**ed** sto**p** – sto**pped** stud**y** – stud**ied** st**ay** – st**ayed**

2 Complete the chart.

Base Form	Past Simple
1. clean	cleaned
2. like	
3. study	
4. play	
5. cook	
6. watch	
7. live	
8. stop	

3 Match A to B to make sentences.

A

1. Laura cleaned
2. We played
3. Harry and Diane danced
4. The students finished
5. School started

B

...... a. football yesterday.
...... b. their homework half an hour ago.
...... c. at nine o'clock yesterday morning.
..1... d. her room at four o'clock.
...... e. at the party on Friday night.

4 Put the words in the correct order to make sentences.

1. called / me / two hours ago / You
   You called me two hours ago.
2. the restaurant / liked / We / last night
   ....
3. worked / yesterday / Alex / in the garden
   ....
4. to my CD / The girls / last week / listened
   ....
5. studied / last year / My friends / French
   ....

5 Complete the sentences with the verbs in brackets. Use the Past Simple affirmative.

1. The teacher ......talked...... (talk) to my parents yesterday.
2. We .... (study) for the test two days ago.
3. Tommy and Ben .... (cook) dinner last night.
4. I .... (wait) for you yesterday.
5. The dog .... (love) my sandwich.

6 Write the sentences in the Past Simple.

1. Mike and Cathy live in France.
   Mike and Cathy lived in France.
2. I watch television in the living room.
   ....
3. Rick and Mandy help their grandmother.
   ....
4. The children play with their friends.
   ....
5. The housekeepers clean the rooms.
   ....

Past Simple: Negative and Questions

1 Read the grammar box.

Negative		Questions		
I you he she it we you they	**did not (didn't) walk**	**Did**	I you he she it we you they	**walk?**
Short Answers: Yes, I **did.** / No, I **didn't.**				

2 Complete the sentences with the verbs in brackets. Use the Past Simple negative.

1. Carol ...*didn't clean*... (clean) her room this morning.
2. The students .... (listen) to the teacher yesterday.
3. I .... (call) the doctor last week.
4. The girls .... (play) basketball after school.
5. Ken .... (like) the hotel.

3 Write the sentences in the negative.

1. I danced at the party last night.
   I didn't dance at the party last night.
2. We studied at the library yesterday.
   ....
3. My father cooked dinner on Tuesday.
   ....
4. Chris and Melissa lived in Turkey last year.
   ....
5. They finished their homework ten minutes ago.
   ....
6. Beth started her project two weeks ago.
   ....

4 Complete the sentences with the verbs in brackets. Use the Past Simple affirmative or negative.

1. Philip ....*helped*..... (help) the receptionist yesterday.
2. I .... (not watch) television last night.
3. We .... (talk) to the electrician five minutes ago.
4. Andrew and Diane .... (not clean) the classroom last week.
5. My mother .... (not play) tennis yesterday afternoon.

5 Put the words in the correct order to make questions.

1. walk / to school / you / yesterday / did
   Did you walk to school yesterday?
2. the lesson / at eight o'clock / did / start
   ....
3. like / her birthday present / did / Abbie
   ....
4. Greg / a question / five minutes ago / did / ask
   ....
   ....
5. the children / did / for you / wait
   ....

6 Match the answers to the questions in Exercise 5.

...... a. Yes, she did.
...... b. No, they didn't.
...... c. Yes, it did.
...... d. Yes, he did.
..*1*.. e. No, I didn't.

UNIT 1

EL PRESENTE DEL VERBO *TO BE*

Afirmativa	Forma Contraída
I **am**	I'**m**
you **are**	you'**re**
he / she / it — **is**	he'**s** she'**s** it'**s**
we / you / they — **are**	we'**re** you'**re** they'**re**

- Este verbo suele traducirse por *ser* o *estar*, pero cuando indicamos la edad se traduce por *tener*.

  *I **am** (I'**m**) a student.* (Yo soy estudiante.)

  *He **is** at school.* (Él está en el colegio.)

  *She **is** 14 years old.* (Ella tiene 14 años.)
- También lo utilizamos para preguntar precios.

  *How much **is** it? It'**s** £5.* (¿Cuánto es? 5 libras.)

Negativa	Forma Contraída
I **am not**	I'**m not**
you **are not**	you **aren't** / you'**re not**
he / she / it — **is not**	he **isn't** / he'**s not** she **isn't** / she'**s not** it **isn't** / it'**s not**
we / you / they — **are not**	we **aren't** / we'**re not** you **aren't** / you'**re not** they **aren't** / they'**re not**

- Para formar una frase en negativa tan solo hay que colocar la partícula **not** detrás del verbo **to be**.
- Como puedes ver en el cuadro, hay dos formas contraídas: una se forma añadiendo la contracción al verbo y otra añadiéndola al pronombre sujeto. Se pueden usar indistintamente, pero recuerda que **not** jamás va contraído con **am**, sólo con **is** y **are**.

  She is English. (Ella es inglesa.)
  *She **is not** (**isn't**) French. / She'**s not** French.*
  (Ella no es francesa.)

  They are teachers. (Son profesores.)
  *They **are not** (**aren't**) doctors. / They'**re not** doctors.* (No son médicos.)

Ejercicio 1

Pon en negativa las siguientes frases.

1. He is Brazilian.
2. We are friends.
3. It is a dictionary.
4. You are Chinese.
5. They are English.

Afirmativa	Interrogativa
I **am**	**Am** I ... ?
you **are**	**Are** you ... ?
he / she / it — **is**	**Is** he ... ? **Is** she ... ? **Is** it ... ?
we / you / they — **are**	**Are** we ... ? **Are** you ... ? **Are** they ... ?

- Para formar la interrogativa con el verbo **to be** ponemos **am**, **is** y **are** delante del sujeto, que puede ser un pronombre personal o un sustantivo. En inglés, el signo de interrogación sólo se pone al final de la pregunta.

  They are Chinese.
  (Ellos son chinos.)
  ***Are** they Chinese?*
  (¿Son chinos?)

  Pierre is from France.
  (Pierre es de Francia.)
  ***Is** Pierre from France?*
  (¿Pierre es de Francia?)

Ejercicio 2

Pon en interrogativa las siguientes frases.

1. Jane is Turkish.
2. You are a student.
3. The teachers are English.
4. I am from Nigeria.
5. She is Mary.

Respuestas Breves	
Afirmativa	**Negativa**
Yes, I **am**.	No, **I'm not**.
Yes, you **are**.	No, you **aren't**.
Yes, he Yes, she — **is**. Yes, it	No, he No, she — **isn't**. No, it
Yes, we Yes, you — **are**. Yes, they	No, we No, you — **aren't**. No, they

- Las respuestas breves son las que damos con un simple *sí* o *no*; pero en inglés, además de **yes** o **no**, necesitan sujeto y verbo. El sujeto siempre es un pronombre personal y el verbo **to be** debe usarse sin contraer en afirmativa pero contraído en negativa.

  *Is the teacher in class? Yes, **he is**. / No, **he isn't**.* (¿Está el profesor en clase? Sí. / No.)

  *Are you French? Yes, **I am**. / No, **I'm not**.* (¿Eres francés? Sí. / No.)

  *Are they ten years old? Yes, **they are**. / No, **they aren't**.* (¿Tienen diez años? Sí. / No.)

Ejercicio 3

Contesta con respuestas breves.

1. Is your name Jane? No, ...
2. Are you English? Yes, ...
3. Is the doctor here? No, ...
4. Are you in London? Yes, ...
5. Is she a teacher? No, ...

Preguntas con partículas interrogativas

- No se pueden contestar con un *sí* o un *no*; requieren una respuesta más completa.

  What? (¿Qué?/¿Cuál?)
  How? (¿Cómo?)
  How often? (¿Con qué frecuencia?)
  Where? (¿Dónde?)
  Who? (¿Quién/es?)

  ***What** is your name?* (¿Cuál es tu nombre? / ¿Cómo te llamas?)
  ***How** are you?* (¿Cómo estás?)
  ***Where** is your friend?* (¿Dónde está tu amigo?)
  ***Who** is the director?* (¿Quién es el director?)

UNIT 2

LOS PRONOMBRES PERSONALES SUJETO

I	(siempre con mayúscula) yo
you	tú, usted
he	él
she	ella
it	ello (no se suele traducir; se usa para referirse a una cosa o animal)
we	nosotros/as
you	vosotros/as, ustedes
they	ellos/as

- Se llaman así porque siempre hacen de sujeto en la oración, y para que esta sea correcta y tenga sentido nunca pueden faltar. Los pronombres personales sujeto siempre van delante del verbo, excepto en las oraciones interrogativas.
- En plural no varían de género; valen igual para el masculino que para el femenino.

  ***I** am the teacher.* (Yo soy el profesor.)

  ***You** are Chinese.* (Tú eres / Usted es chino.)

  *Peter is a man. **He** is from France.* (Peter es un hombre. Él es de Francia.)

  *Mary is a woman. **She** is English.* (Mary es una mujer. Ella es inglesa.)

  *France is a country. **It** is next to Spain.* (Francia es un país. Está al lado de España.)

  ***We** are students.* (Nosotras somos estudiantes.)

  ***You** are tall.* (Vosotros sois / Ustedes son altos.)

  *My friends are here. **They** are Brazilian.* (Mis amigos están aquí. Ellos son brasileños.)

LOS ADJETIVOS POSESIVOS

my	mi, mis
your	tu, tus, su, sus (de usted)
his	su, sus (de él)
her	su, sus (de ella)
its	su, sus (de cosa o animal)
our	nuestro/a, nuestros/as
your	vuestro/a, vuestros/as, su, sus (de ustedes)
their	su, sus (de ellos/as)

- Van delante del nombre que indica lo que poseemos, sin importar que sea una cosa o varias pues son iguales en singular y en plural.
- Por su forma es fácil saber quién es el poseedor, sobre todo en la 3ª persona del singular ya que **his** indica un poseedor masculino, **her** uno femenino e **its** uno neutro (cosa o animal).

  ***my** pencil* (mi lápiz)
  ***my** friends* (mis amigas)
  ***your** address* (tu dirección, su dirección [de usted])
  ***your** teachers* (tus profesores, sus profesores [de usted])
  ***his** sister* (su hermana [de él])
  ***his** brothers* (sus hermanos [de él])
  ***her** watch* (su reloj [de ella])
  ***her** jackets* (sus chaquetas [de ella])
  ***its** food* (su comida)
  ***its** eyes* (sus ojos)
  ***our** school* (nuestro colegio)
  ***our** classes* (nuestras clases)
  ***your** bike* (vuestra bici, su bici [de ustedes])
  ***your** books* (vuestros libros, sus libros [de ustedes])
  ***their** car* (su coche [de ellos/as])
  ***their** chairs* (sus sillas [de ellos/as])

Ejercicio 4
Traduce.

1. Mi trabajo.	5. Nuestro camarero.
2. Tu médico.	6. Sus libros (de ellas).
3. Su nombre (de él).	7. Vuestra profesora.
4. Su lápiz (de ella).	8. Su nombre (de animal).

A / AN

- El artículo indefinido **a** / **an** va delante de un nombre contable en singular y se traduce por *un, una*. La única diferencia que hay entre los dos es que **an** se usa cuando la siguiente palabra empieza por vocal o por **h** muda.

  *I've got **a** book.*
  (Tengo un libro.)

  *She's got **an** ice cream.*
  (Ella tiene un helado.)

  ***An** hour has got sixty minutes.*
  (Una hora tiene sesenta minutos.)

EL PLURAL DE LOS NOMBRES

El plural regular

- Se forma añadiendo una **s** al nombre singular.

  book — *book**s***
  pencil — *pencil**s***
  computer — *computer**s***

- Si el nombre singular acaba en **consonante** + **y**, cambia la **y** por **i** y añade las letras **es**.

  *countr**y*** — *countr**ies***
  *dictionar**y*** — *dictionar**ies***

- Pero si acaba en **vocal** + **y** sólo se añade la **s**.

  *da**y*** — *day**s***
  *bo**y*** — *boy**s***

Los plurales irregulares

- Algunos nombres forman el plural sin seguir ninguna regla y hay que aprenderlos de memoria.

  child (niño/a) — ***children*** (niños/as)
  man (hombre) — ***men*** (hombres)
  woman (mujer) — ***women*** (mujeres)

THIS / THAT / THESE / THOSE

- Son pronombres demostrativos que se refieren al nombre que va detrás del verbo **to be**.
- **This** indica algo singular y cercano, y significa *este, esta, esto*. **That** señala algo singular pero que está lejos, y por tanto significa *ese, esa, eso* o *aquel, aquella, aquello*.

  ***This is** my mother.*
  (Esta es mi madre.) [está a tu lado]
  ***That is** my favourite restaurant.*
  (Aquel es mi restaurante favorito.) [lo señalas en la distancia]

- **These** indica algo plural y cercano, y se traduce por *estos, estas*, mientras que **those** indica algo plural y lejano y por tanto significa *esos, esas* o *aquellos, aquellas*.

  ***These are** my books.* (Estos son mis libros.)
  ***Those are** our houses.* (Esas son nuestras casas.)

- Cuando funcionan como adjetivos demostrativos van delante de un nombre. Entonces **this** y **that** no pueden traducirse como *esto, eso* o *aquello*.

  ***This** actress is French.*
  (Esta actriz es francesa.)
  ***That** man is sad.*
  (Ese hombre está triste.)

These toys are new.
(Estos juguetes son nuevos.)
Those women are shop assistants.
(Esas mujeres son dependientas de una tienda.)

Ejercicio 5

Traduce.

1. Esto es un libro.
2. Esta mujer es inglesa.
3. Aquello es una mesa.
4. Aquellos son libros.
5. Estos son números.
6. Aquellas son recepcionistas.

UNIT 3

EL VERBO *HAVE GOT*

Afirmativa	Forma Contraída
I / you — **have got**	I**'ve got** / you**'ve got**
he / she / it — **has got**	he**'s got** / she**'s got** / it**'s got**
we / you / they — **have got**	we**'ve got** / you**'ve got** / they**'ve got**

- Significa *tener* y sirve para expresar lo que poseemos o las características de alguien o algo cuando lo describimos.

  *I **have got** (I**'ve got**) a cat.* (Tengo un gato.)

  *She **has got** (She**'s got**) blue eyes.* (Tiene los ojos azules.)

Negativa	Forma Contraída
I / you — **have not got**	I / you — **haven't got**
he / she / it — **has not got**	he / she / it — **hasn't got**
we / you / they — **have not got**	we / you / they — **haven't got**

- En negativa añadimos **not** o **n't** a **have** y **has**.

  *I **have not (haven't) got** a chair.*
  (No tengo silla.)
  *He **has not (hasn't) got** a girlfriend.*
  (Él no tiene novia.)

Afirmativa	Interrogativa
I / you — **have got**	**Have** I **got** ... ? / **Have** you **got** ... ?
he / she / it — **has got**	**Has** he **got** ... ? / **Has** she **got** ... ? / **Has** it **got** ... ?
we / you / they — **have got**	**Have** we **got** ... ? / **Have** you **got** ... ? / **Have** they **got** ... ?

- En interrogativa se coloca **have** / **has** delante del sujeto.

  ***Have** you **got** three sisters?*
  (¿Tienes tres hermanas?)

  ***Has** Pam **got** a red car?*
  (¿Tiene Pam un coche rojo?)

Ejercicio 6

Traduce.

1. Tenemos un amigo.
2. ¿Tienes hermanos y hermanas?
3. No tengo ordenador.
4. ¿Tenéis una hermana?
5. Ella no tiene teléfono.

Respuestas Breves	
Afirmativa	**Negativa**
Yes, I / Yes, you — **have.**	No, I / No, you — **haven't.**
Yes, he / Yes, she / Yes, it — **has.**	No, he / No, she / No, it — **hasn't.**
Yes, we / Yes, you / Yes, they — **have.**	No, we / No, you / No, they — **haven't.**

- Para contestar brevemente a las preguntas con **have got** se usa **yes** o **no**, y luego el pronombre personal sujeto y **have** / **has** o **haven't** / **hasn't** (sin **got**).

  ***Have** you **got** a grandchild? Yes, **I have**.*
  (¿Tienes un nieto? Sí.)

  ***Have** you **got** two aunts? No, **I haven't**.*
  (¿Tienes dos tías? No.)

  ***Has** your father **got** a sister? Yes, **he has**.*
  (¿Tiene tu padre una hermana? Sí.)

  ***Has** this class **got** a computer? No, **it hasn't**.*
  (¿Tiene un ordenador esta clase? No.)

Ejercicio 7

Contesta con respuestas breves.

1. Have you got three sisters? No, ...
2. Have Mary and John got a radio? Yes, ...
3. Has Peter got a wife? Yes, ...
4. Has Jane got a boyfriend? No, ...
5. Has the house got four bedrooms? Yes, ...

LOS NOMBRES CONTABLES Y LOS NO CONTABLES

- Los nombres contables, que se pueden contar, tienen singular y plural y pueden llevar delante un artículo (**a**, **an**, **some**, **the**) o un numeral: *a snake, an eye, some children, the teacher, three chairs...*
- Los nombres no contables no se pueden contar porque se refieren a sustancias y cosas abstractas; sólo tienen singular y pueden llevar delante **some**.

  coffee — ***some** coffee*
  homework — ***some** homework*

SOME / ANY

- **Some** sólo se utiliza en oraciones afirmativas. Delante de nombres contables en plural significa *unos/as, algunos/as*, pero delante de nombres no contables significa *un poco de, algo de*. A veces puede no traducirse.

  *I've got **some** pencils.*
  (Tengo [unos / algunos] lápices.)

  *She's got **some** money.*
  (Tiene [un poco de] dinero.)
- **Any** acompaña a nombres contables en plural y a no contables. Significa *ningún/una, nada de* en las oraciones negativas, pero *algún/una, algunos/as, algo de* en las interrogativas. Puede no traducirse.

  *I haven't got **any** brothers.*
  (No tengo hermanos / ningún hermano.)

  *Have you got **any** pets?*
  (¿Tienes mascotas / alguna mascota?)

Ejercicio 8

Traduce.

1. Tengo una televisión.
2. No tengo ninguna amiga.
3. ¿Tienes algún hermano?
4. No tenemos una recepcionista.
5. ¿Tienes alguna tía?

EL GENITIVO SAJÓN

El genitivo sajón con singular

- Se usa para indicar de quién es algo. Para ello añadimos un apóstrofo (') y una **s** al poseedor.

  *my **father's** watch* (el reloj de mi padre)
  *my **uncle's** wife* (la esposa de mi tío)
  *the **teacher's** book* (el libro del profesor)
- Si utilizamos el nombre propio del poseedor, no ponemos artículo.

  ***Emily's** bedroom* (el dormitorio de Emily)
- Si el nombre del poseedor acaba en **s** sólo le añadimos el apóstrofo (o las dos cosas, aunque lo más frecuente es la primera opción).

  ***James'** coat / **James's** coat* (el abrigo de James)
- Si hay más de un poseedor, sólo añadimos el apóstrofo y la **s** al segundo.

  ***John and Mary's** house is big.*
  (La casa de John y Mary es grande.)
- Con las cosas se usa la preposición **of** en vez del genitivo sajón.

  *the name **of** the street* (el nombre de la calle)
  ~~*the street's name*~~

Ejercicio 9

Traduce.

1. La hermana de Luis.
2. El pelo de tu hermana.
3. El diccionario de mi profesor.
4. El libro de mi amigo.
5. El dormitorio de Thomas.

El genitivo sajón con plural

- Si el nombre del poseedor es plural y termina en **s**, sólo se pone el apóstrofo, pero si es un plural irregular, añadimos apóstrofo y **s**.

  *the **boys'** notebooks* (los cuadernos de los chicos)
  *the **women's** husbands* (los maridos de las mujeres)

Ejercicio 10

Traduce.

1. La habitación de los niños.
2. La casa de mis amigos.
3. Los libros de las niñas.
4. El examen de los estudiantes.
5. Los coches de los hombres.

EL ORDEN DE LOS ADJETIVOS EN LA ORACIÓN

- Los adjetivos en inglés van colocados delante del nombre y no varían de género ni de número; es decir, tienen la misma forma en masculino y femenino, singular y plural.

  *the **small** chair* (la silla pequeña)
  *the **small** dogs* (los perros pequeños)

- También pueden ir colocados después del verbo **to be**.

  *This bed is **old**.*
  (Esta cama es vieja.)
  *That boy is **good-looking**.*
  (Ese chico es guapo.)

Ejercicio 11
Traduce.
1. Tu nombre es bonito.
2. Mi coche es grande.
3. Los niños son buenos.
4. Nuestra hija es guapa.
5. Mi padre es guapo.
6. Tengo un hijo alto.
7. Nuestro profesor está delgado.
8. Nuestra casa tiene habitaciones pequeñas.
9. Mi madre tiene el pelo corto.
10. Este es un libro fantástico.

THERE IS / THERE ARE

Afirmativa	Forma Contraída
There is	There's
There are	–

- **There is** significa que hay una cosa y por eso va seguido de un nombre contable en singular o de un nombre no contable.
- **There are** significa que hay dos cosas o más y sólo puede ir con nombres contables en plural.

  ***There is** (**There's**) a snake.*
  (Hay una serpiente.)
  ***There is** (**There's**) some water in the bottle.*
  (Hay agua en la botella.)
  ***There are** three girls in the cinema.*
  (Hay tres chicas en el cine.)

Negativa	Forma Contraída
There is not	There isn't
There are not	There aren't

- La negativa se forma añadiendo **not** o **n't** detrás de **is** / **are**.

  ***There is not** (**isn't**) a park near here.*
  (No hay ningún parque cerca de aquí.)
  ***There is not** (**isn't**) any apple juice in the fridge.*
  (No hay zumo de manzana en el frigorífico.)
  ***There are not** (**aren't**) any chairs in the library.*
  (No hay ninguna silla en la biblioteca.)

Interrogativa	Respuestas Breves
Is there... ?	Yes, **there is.** / No, **there isn't.**
Are there... ?	Yes, **there are.** / No, **there aren't.**

- Las preguntas empiezan con **is** o **are**, pero en las respuestas breves volvemos al orden normal y, si son negativas, usamos las formas contraídas.

  ***Is there** a ball? Yes, **there is**. /*
  *No, **there isn't**.* (¿Hay un balón? Sí. / No.)
  ***Is there** any homework? Yes, **there is**. /*
  *No, **there isn't**.* (¿Hay deberes? Sí. / No.)
  ***Are there** books here? Yes, **there are**. /*
  *No, **there aren't**.* (¿Hay libros aquí? Sí. / No.)

Ejercicio 12
Traduce.
1. Hay un escritorio en el dormitorio.
2. Hay diez estudiantes en la clase.
3. No hay nada de dinero aquí.
4. No hay sillas en la cocina.
5. ¿Hay un bolígrafo encima del escritorio?
6. ¿Hay algún gato aquí?

HOW MUCH / HOW MANY

- Usamos estas dos expresiones para preguntar por la cantidad de algo que queremos saber.
- **How much**? (¿Cuánto/a?) sólo se usa delante de nombres no contables.

  ***How much** orange juice is there?*
  (¿Cuánto zumo de naranja hay?)

- Si no va seguido de un nombre sino del verbo **to be**, es para preguntar el precio de una cosa.

  ***How much** is the jacket?*
  (¿Cuánto cuesta la chaqueta?)
- **How many**? (¿Cuántos/as?) sólo va con nombres contables en plural.

  ***How many** pets have you got?*
  (¿Cuántas mascotas tienes?)

Ejercicio 13

Completa las preguntas con *How much* o *How many*.

1. ... children have you got?
2. ... coffee is there?
3. ... books have you got?
4. ... homework have we got?
5. ... is this table?

UNIT 5

EL *PRESENT SIMPLE* EN AFIRMATIVA

Afirmativa	Traducción
I / you — **walk**	ando / andas
he / she / it — **walks**	él anda / ella anda / anda
we / you / they — **walk**	andamos / andáis / andan

- El *Present Simple* se usa para expresar hechos habituales, situaciones y estados.

  *I **start** school at nine o'clock.*
  (Entro al colegio a las nueve.)

  *We usually **run** in the afternoon.*
  (Normalmente corremos por la tarde.)

  *They **get up** late on Sundays.*
  (Ellos se levantan tarde los domingos.)
- **Muy importante:** la tercera persona del singular añade una **s** al final.

  *She live**s** in a flat.* (Ella vive en un piso.)

  *She work**s** in the morning.* (Ella trabaja por la mañana.)
- Sin embargo, los siguientes verbos añaden **es**:
  - Los acabados en **consonante** + **y**, que además cambian la **y** por **i**.

    *stud**y*** *stud**ies***
  - Los terminados en ***ch***.

    *tea**ch*** *teach**es***
  - Los que acaban en ***o***.

    *g**o*** *go**es***
- No olvides nunca poner el sujeto en inglés, bien sea nombre o pronombre, aunque este último rara vez se traduzca.

  ***Jack** studies English.* (Jack estudia inglés.)
  ***I** dance.* (Yo bailo. / Bailo.)

Ejercicio 14

Traduce.

1. Yo vivo en Brighton.
2. Estudiamos en el colegio.
3. Ella ve la tele los viernes.
4. Ellos trabajan en el hospital.
5. Me levanto pronto.

EL VERBO *LIKE* + SUSTANTIVO

- Para expresar gustos y preferencias se utiliza el verbo **like** (gustar) seguido de un nombre.

  *I **like** chocolate.* (Me gusta el chocolate.)
  *He **likes** fruit.* (Le gusta la fruta.)
- Para poner este verbo en negativa utiliza **don't** / **doesn't**, y para la interrogativa recuerda poner **do** / **does** delante del sujeto.

  *I **don't like** this song.*
  (No me gusta esta canción.)

  *She **doesn't like** animals.*
  (A ella no le gustan los animales.)

  ***Do** you **like** books?*
  (¿Te gustan los libros?)

  ***Does** he **like** Italian food?*
  (¿Le gusta la comida italiana?)

Ejercicio 15

Traduce.

1. Les gusta la música.
2. Me gustan los jardines.
3. A él le gusta Londres.
4. Te gustan los pósters de animales.
5. A ella le gusta la comida china.

EL VERBO *LIKE* + VERBO + *ING*

- Para indicar lo que nos gusta o no nos gusta hacer utilizamos el verbo **like** seguido de un verbo terminado en **ing**.

  I ***like doing*** *sport.*
  (Me gusta hacer deporte.)

  He ***doesn't like speaking*** *in class.*
  (No le gusta hablar en clase.)

  Do *you* ***like listening*** *to music?*
  (¿Te gusta escuchar música?)

Ejercicio 16

Traduce.

1. Me gusta leer libros.
2. A Jack le gusta jugar al fútbol.
3. Te gusta estudiar inglés.
4. Nos gusta vivir en Londres.
5. Me gusta escuchar música.

UNIT 6

LOS ADVERBIOS DE FRECUENCIA

- Son palabras muy usadas con el *Present Simple* porque expresan la frecuencia con que hacemos algo. Los principales son estos:

  always (siempre)

  usually (normalmente)

  often (a menudo)

  sometimes (a veces, algunas veces)

  never (nunca)

- Siempre van entre el sujeto y el verbo, excepto cuando es el verbo **to be**, en cuyo caso los adverbios van detrás de él.

  He ***usually goes*** *to bed at ten o'clock.*
  (Él normalmente se acuesta a las diez.)

  I ***am never*** *late.* (Nunca llego tarde.)

LET´S + VERBO

- **Let's** seguido de un verbo en su forma base se usa para hacer sugerencias.

  Let's *dance.* (Vamos a bailar. / Bailemos.)
  Let's *work.* (Vamos a trabajar. / Trabajemos.)

Ejercicio 17

Traduce.

1. Vamos a cocinar.
2. Leamos un libro.
3. Veamos la tele.
4. Bailemos ahora.
5. Vamos a cenar en un restaurante.

EL *PRESENT SIMPLE* EN NEGATIVA E INTERROGATIVA

Negativa		Forma Contraída	
I / you	do not walk	I / you	don't walk
he / she / it	does not walk	he / she / it	doesn't walk
we / you / they	do not walk	we / you / they	don't walk

- Con **I**, **you**, **we** y **they** la negativa del *Present Simple* se forma poniendo **do not** delante del verbo en la forma base. En la conversación se usa más la forma contraída **don't**.

  I like tea. (Me gusta el té.)
  I ***do not (don't) like*** *tea.* (No me gusta el té.)

  You study French. (Estudias francés.)
  You ***do not (don't)*** **study** *French.* (No estudias francés.)

  We read books. (Leemos libros.)
  We ***do not (don't) read*** *books.* (No leemos libros.)

  They live in Bristol. (Viven en Bristol.)
  They ***do not (don't) live*** *in Bristol.* (No viven en Bristol.)

- Con **he**, **she** e **it** la negativa se forma con **does not** o la contracción **doesn't** y el verbo en la forma base. Fíjate en cómo pierde la **s** que añade en afirmativa.

  He speaks German. (Él habla alemán.)
  He ***does not (doesn't) speak*** *German.* (Él no habla alemán.)

  My mother works in an office. (Mi madre trabaja en una oficina.)
  My mother ***does not (doesn't) work*** *in an office.* (Mi madre no trabaja en una oficina.)

  It sleeps on the sofa. (Duerme en el sofá.)
  It ***does not (doesn't) sleep*** *on the sofa.* (No duerme en el sofá.)

Ejercicio 18

Pon en negativa las siguientes frases.

1. I work here.
2. He lives in Paris.
3. My mother works in a restaurant.
4. I like this colour.
5. My friend likes my house.
6. My father listens to the radio.

Interrogativa			Traducción
Do	I you	**walk?**	¿Ando? ¿Andas?
Does	he she it	**walk?**	¿Él anda? ¿Ella anda? ¿Anda?
Do	we you they	**walk?**	¿Andamos? ¿Andáis? ¿Andan?

- Con **I**, **you**, **we** y **they** la interrogativa se forma poniendo **do** delante del sujeto.

  I study in the evenings.
  (Estudio por las tardes.)
  ***Do** I **study** in the evenings?*
  (¿Estudio por las tardes?)

  They live on the third floor.
  (Ellos viven en el tercer piso.)
  ***Do** they **live** on the third floor?*
  (¿Viven en el tercer piso?)

- Con **he**, **she** e **it** la interrogativa se forma con **does**, y como este verbo auxiliar ya está en 3ª persona del singular, el verbo principal se pone en la forma base.

  He eats sausages. (Él come salchichas.)
  ***Does** he **eat** sausages?* (¿Él come salchichas?)

- Los verbos **to be** y **have got** no necesitan **do** / **does** en negativa ni en interrogativa.

  ***Is** your birthday in June?* (¿Es tu cumpleaños en junio?)
  ***Have** you **got** my pencil?* (¿Tienes mi lápiz?)

Ejercicio 19

Pon en interrogativa las siguientes frases.

1. I love my boyfriend.
2. He likes my flat.
3. Her father lives in Rome.
4. We study English.
5. His family has breakfast in the kitchen.

Respuestas Breves			
Afirmativa		Negativa	
Yes, I Yes, you	**do.**	No, I No, you	**don't.**
Yes, he Yes, she Yes, it	**does.**	No, he No, she No, it	**doesn't.**
Yes, we Yes, you Yes, they	**do.**	No, we No, you No, they	**don't.**

- En las respuestas breves se usa el pronombre sujeto y **do** o **does** si son afirmativas o **don't** y **doesn't** si son negativas.

  ***Do** you **watch** TV? Yes, **I do**. / No, **I don't**.*
  (¿Ves la televisión? Sí. / No.)

  ***Does** she **go** to the cinema? Yes, **she does**. / No, **she doesn't**.* (¿Ella va al cine? Sí. / No.)

Preguntas con partículas interrogativas

- Para hacer preguntas en *Present Simple* con las partículas interrogativas **who**, **what**, **where**, **when**, **how**, **how often**, etc., ponemos la partícula en primer lugar, y a continuación **do** o **does** seguido del sujeto y del verbo en la forma base.

  ***What do** you **do** at 6 pm? I listen to music.*
  (¿Qué haces a las 18:00? Escucho música.)

  ***How does** she **go** to work? She goes by car.*
  (¿Cómo va a trabajar? Ella va en coche.)

  ***How often do** you **go** to the cinema? Every day.* (¿Con qué frecuencia vas al cine? Todos los días.)

- En el caso de **to be** y **have got**, como no llevan **do** / **does** en las preguntas, sólo ponemos la partícula interrogativa al principio e invertimos el orden del sujeto y el verbo.

  ***When is** your birthday?*
  (¿Cuándo es tu cumpleaños?)

  ***What have** you **got** in your hand?*
  (¿Qué tienes en la mano?)

Ejercicio 20

Traduce.

1. ¿Dónde estudia Helen? Estudia en mi casa.
2. ¿Dónde coméis? Comemos en la oficina.
3. ¿Qué os gusta? Nos gusta la música.
4. ¿Cuándo se acuestan? A las 22:30.
5. ¿Qué hacen los niños? Ellos leen libros.

UNIT 7

CAN

- Es un verbo que se utiliza para expresar habilidad (saber) y posibilidad (poder).
- En la 3ª persona del singular no añade **s** y siempre va seguido de otro verbo en la forma base.

  *I **can come** to the party.*
  (Puedo venir a la fiesta.)

  *My mother **can drive**.*
  (Mi madre sabe conducir.)

  *They **can speak** Chinese.*
  (Ellos saben hablar chino.)

- En negativa sólo se le añade **not**, sin separación, o se usa la forma contraída **can't**.

  *I **cannot** / **can't cook**.* (No sé cocinar.)

  *He **cannot** / **can't walk**.* (Él no puede andar.)

- Para hacer preguntas tan solo hay que colocar **can** delante del sujeto. En las respuestas breves se vuelve al orden normal, usando el pronombre sujeto y **can** o **can't**, según sean afirmativas o negativas.

  ***Can** they **go** to the bank? Yes, **they can**. / No, **they can't**.* (¿Pueden ir al banco? Sí. / No.)

  ***Can** you **swim**? Yes, **I can**. / No, **I can't**.*
  (¿Sabes nadar? Sí. / No.)

- También utilizamos **can** en preguntas para pedir permiso.

  ***Can** I **go** to the park?* (¿Puedo ir al parque?)

Ejercicio 21

Traduce.

1. Sé cocinar.
2. Lisa no sabe hablar inglés.
3. Podemos cenar en un restaurante.
4. Ellos no saben conducir.
5. ¿Puedes venir a la fiesta?

LAS PREPOSICIONES DE TIEMPO *ON, IN, AT*

- Utilizamos **on** con los nombres de los días de la semana (los cuales siempre se escriben con mayúscula en inglés) y en otras expresiones.

  ***on** Tuesday* (el martes)

  ***on** Tuesday morning* (el martes por la mañana)

  ***on** my birthday* (en mi cumpleaños)

- Usamos **in** con las partes del día, los meses (que también se escriben con mayúscula) y los años.

  ***in** the morning / afternoon / evening*
  (por la mañana / tarde)
  Excepción: ***at** night* (por la noche)

  ***in** May* (en mayo)
  ***in** 2006* (en 2006)

- Usamos **at** con las horas y otras expresiones.

  ***at** 5 o'clock* (a las cinco en punto)
  ***at** the weekend* (el fin de semana)
  ***at** midday* (a mediodía)
  ***at** midnight* (a medianoche)

Ejercicio 22

Traduce.

1. Tengo una fiesta en mayo.
2. Mis padres van de compras los lunes.
3. Mi cumpleaños es en junio.
4. Tengo clase de inglés por la mañana.
5. Tengo clase de inglés el viernes por la mañana.

UNIT 8

EL *PRESENT CONTINUOUS*

Afirmativa	Forma Contraída
I **am talking**	I**'m talking**
you **are talking**	you**'re talking**
he / she / it — **is talking**	he / she / it — **'s talking**
we / you / they — **are talking**	we / you / they — **'re talking**

- El *Present Continuous* expresa acciones que están ocurriendo en el momento mismo de hablar o en el periodo de tiempo presente.
- La afirmativa se forma con el presente del verbo **to be** como auxiliar y el verbo principal terminado en **ing**.

  *I **am** (I'**m**) **reading** a book in English.*
  (Estoy leyendo un libro en inglés.)

  *She **is** (She'**s**) **watching** the football match.*
  (Ella está viendo el partido de fútbol.)

  *They **are** (They'**re**) **listening** to music.*
  (Están escuchando música.)

Ejercicio 23

Traduce.

1. Ahora estamos leyendo un libro.
2. Ahora estoy desayunando.
3. Ella está corriendo ahora mismo.
4. Están bailando.
5. En este momento Tom está durmiendo.

Negativa	Forma Contraída
I **am not talking**	I**'m not talking**
you **are not talking**	you **aren't talking**
he / she / it **is not talking**	he / she / it **isn't talking**
we / you / they **are not talking**	we / you / they **aren't talking**

- En negativa se pone la partícula **not** entre el verbo **to be** (que al hablar suele contraerse) y el terminado en **ing**.

  The phone ***is not (isn't) ringing****.*
  (El teléfono no está sonando.)
  We ***are not (aren't) sleeping****.*
  (No estamos durmiendo.)

Ejercicio 24

Pon en negativa las siguientes frases.

1. She is dancing.
2. I am studying right now.
3. You're cooking.
4. They're talking now.
5. He's watching TV.

Interrogativa	Respuestas Breves Afirmativa / Negativa
Am I / Are you **talking?**	Yes, I **am**. / No, I**'m not**. Yes, you **are**. / No, you **aren't**.
Is he / Is she / Is it **talking?**	Yes, he **is**. / No, he **isn't**. Yes, she **is**. / No, she **isn't**. Yes, it **is**. / No, it **isn't**.
Are we / Are you / Are they **talking?**	Yes, we **are**. / No, we **aren't**. Yes, you **are**. / No, you **aren't**. Yes, they **are**. / No, they **aren't**.

- En interrogativa se intercala el sujeto entre el verbo **to be** y el terminado en **ing**. En las respuestas breves afirmativas se usa el pronombre sujeto y **am**, **is** o **are** sin contraer, pero en las negativas sí se contraen.

  Are *you* ***talking*** *to your friends? Yes,* ***I am****.*
  (¿Estás hablando con tus amigos? Sí.)

  Is *he* ***buying*** *bread? No,* ***he isn't****.*
  (¿Está comprando pan? No.)

Ejercicio 25

Pon en interrogativa las siguientes frases.

1. We're sleeping.
2. You're singing.
3. They are reading books.
4. She's cleaning her bedroom.
5. He is writing an e-mail.

- Antes de añadir la terminación **ing** a la forma base hay que seguir estas reglas ortográficas, dependiendo de cómo sea el verbo:
  - Si acaba en **e** muda, pierde esa vocal.
    *come - com****ing*** *write - writ****ing***
  - Si tiene una sílaba y acaba en **1 vocal + 1 consonante**, dobla esa consonante.
    *sit - sit****ting*** *swim - swim****ming***
- Con el *Present Continuous* se utilizan las siguientes expresiones temporales: **now** (ahora), **right now** (justo ahora, ahora mismo), **at the moment** (en este momento), **today** (hoy), **this morning** (esta mañana), etc. Todas pueden ir al principio o al final de la frase, pero se suelen poner al final.

  We ***are studying*** *English* ***now****.*
  (Ahora estamos estudiando inglés.)

GLOSSARY

Pronunciation Key

ɑ:	start, arm	ɪə	near	d	did	t	tea
æ	act, hat	ɒ	lot	f	fit	v	voice
aɪ	cry, five	əʊ	note, coat	g	good	w	win
aɪə	fire, tyre	ɔ:	more, saw	h	how	z	zoo
aʊ	out, down	ɔɪ	boy, coin	j	yellow	ʃ	shop, action
aʊə	flour, tower	ʊ	could, stood	k	king, cat	ʒ	measure, vision
e	met, lend	u:	you, choose	l	leg	ŋ	ring
eɪ	say, main, weight	ʊə	sure	m	man	tʃ	cheap
eə	fair, care, wear	ɜ:	turn, third, word	n	no	θ	thanks
ɪ	fit	ʌ	but, must	p	pen	ð	the
i:	feed, beat	ə	forgotten, ago	r	run	dʒ	June
i	happy	b	bed	s	soon		

Todos los significados dados en este glosario corresponden estrictamente al contexto en el que aparecen las palabras en el libro. Este glosario no debe nunca sustituir a un diccionario.

A

a long time /ə lɒŋ 'taɪm/ mucho tiempo
actor /'æktə/ actor
actress /'æktrəs/ actriz
address /ə'dres/ dirección
advertisement /əd'vɜ:tɪsmənt/ anuncio
age /eɪdʒ/ edad
already /ɔ:l'redi/ ya
always /'ɔ:lweɪz/ siempre
any more /eni 'mɔ:/ ya no más, ya no
April /'eɪprəl/ abril
arm /ɑ:m/ brazo
at the moment /æt ðə 'məʊmənt/ en este momento
August /'ɔ:gəst/ agosto
aunt /ɑ:nt/ tía
average /'ævərɪdʒ/ normal, típico/a

B

babysitter /'beɪbisɪtə/ niñera, canguro
bakery /'beɪkəri/ panadería
ball /bɔ:l/ balón, pelota
bananas /bə'nɑ:nəz/ plátanos
bank /bæŋk/ banco
banknotes /'bæŋknəʊts/ billetes (dinero)
bat /bæt/ bate
bathroom /'bɑ:θru:m/ cuarto de baño
beautiful /'bju:tɪfl/ guapo/a, bonito/a
because /bɪ'kɒz/ porque
bed /bed/ cama
bedroom /'bedru:m/ dormitorio
big /bɪg/ grande
birthday /'bɜ:θdeɪ/ cumpleaños
black /blæk/ negro/a
blond /blɒnd/ rubio
blonde /blɒnd/ rubia
blue /blu:/ azul
board /bɔ:d/ pizarra
body /'bɒdi/ cuerpo
book /bʊk/ libro
bookshelves /'bʊkʃelvz/ estanterías para libros
boring /'bɔ:rɪŋ/ aburrido/a (que aburre)
boyfriend /'bɔɪfrend/ novio
Brazil /brə'zɪl/ Brasil
Brazilian /brə'zɪliən/ brasileño/a
bricks /brɪks/ ladrillos
brother /'brʌðə/ hermano
brown /braʊn/ marrón; castaño/a
build /bɪld/ construir
buy /baɪ/ comprar

C

cake /keɪk/ tarta, pastel
call /kɔ:l/ llamar por teléfono
car /kɑ:/ coche

cat /kæt/ gato/a

chain /tʃeɪn/ cadena

chair /tʃeə/ silla

chicken /'tʃɪkɪn/ pollo

child /tʃaɪld/ niño/a, hijo/a

children /'tʃɪldrən/ niños/as, hijos/as

China /'tʃaɪnə/ China

Chinese /tʃaɪ'ni:z/ chino/a

chips /tʃɪps/ patatas fritas

cinema /'sɪnəmə/ cine

clean /kli:n/ limpiar

clothes shop /'kləʊðz ʃɒp/ tienda de ropa

club /klʌb/ club, discoteca

computer /kəm'pju:tə/ ordenador

cook (n) /kʊk/ cocinero/a

cook (v) /kʊk/ cocinar

cooker /'kʊkə/ cocina (electrodoméstico)

cupboard /'kʌbəd/ armario

customer /'kʌstəmə/ cliente/a

D

dance /dɑ:ns/ bailar

dark /dɑ:k/ oscuro/a

daughter /'dɔ:tə/ hija

December /dɪ'sembə/ diciembre

department store /dɪ'pɑ:tmənt stɔ:/ grandes almacenes

desk /desk/ escritorio

dictionary /'dɪkʃənri/ diccionario

dining room /'daɪnɪŋ ru:m/ comedor

doctor /'dɒktə/ médico/a, doctor/a

dog /dɒg/ perro/a

Don't worry /dəʊnt 'wʌri/ No te preocupes / se preocupe

dress /dres/ vestido

drive /draɪv/ conducir; llevar (a alguien) en coche

E

ear /ɪə/ oreja

early /'ɜ:li/ pronto, temprano

eat /i:t/ comer

egg /eg/ huevo

eight /eɪt/ ocho

eighteen /eɪ'ti:n/ dieciocho

eighth /eɪtθ/ octavo/a

eighty /'eɪti/ ochenta

electrician /ɪlek'trɪʃn/ electricista

eleven /ɪ'levn/ once

eleventh /ɪ'levnθ/ undécimo/a

England /'ɪŋglənd/ Inglaterra

English /'ɪŋglɪʃ/ inglés/esa

English-speaking /'ɪŋglɪʃ spi:kɪŋ/ de habla inglesa

everyone /'evriwʌn/ todo el mundo

Excuse me /ɪk'skju:z mi:/ Perdona/e

eye /aɪ/ ojo

F

family /'fæməli/ familia (~ *tree*: árbol genealógico)

fantastic /fæn'tæstɪk/ fantástico/a

fast (adj) /fɑ:st/ rápido/a

fast (adv) /fɑ:st/ deprisa

fat /fæt/ gordo/a

father /'fɑ:ðə/ padre

February /'februəri/ febrero

fifteen /fɪf'ti:n/ quince

fifth /fɪfθ/ quinto/a

fifty /'fɪfti/ cincuenta

find /faɪnd/ encontrar

Fine, thanks /'faɪn θæŋks/ Bien, gracias

finger /'fɪŋgə/ dedo de la mano

finish school /fɪnɪʃ 'sku:l/ salir de clase

first /fɜ:st/ primero/a

fish /fɪʃ/ pez; pescado

five /faɪv/ cinco

flat /flæt/ piso, apartamento

floor /flɔ:/ planta (de un edificio)

food /fu:d/ comida

foot /fʊt/ pie

football match /'fʊtbɔ:l mætʃ/ partido de fútbol

for sale /fə 'seɪl/ en venta, se vende

form /fɔ:m/ formulario

forty /'fɔ:ti/ cuarenta

four /fɔ:/ cuatro

fourteen /fɔ:'ti:n/ catorce

fourth /fɔ:θ/ cuarto/a

France /frɑ:ns/ Francia

French /frentʃ/ francés/esa

Friday /'fraɪdeɪ/ viernes

fridge /frɪdʒ/ frigorífico

friends /frendz/ amigos/as

G

game /geɪm/ juego; partido

garage /'gærɑ:ʒ/ garaje

garden /'gɑ:dn/ jardín

get home /get 'həʊm/ llegar a casa

get up /get 'ʌp/ levantarse

girlfriend /'gɜːlfrend/ novia

go /gəʊ/ ir

go out /gəʊ 'aʊt/ salir

go shopping /gəʊ 'ʃɒpɪŋ/ ir de compras

go to bed /'gəʊ tə bed/ acostarse

Good afternoon /gʊd ɑːftə'nuːn/ Buenas tardes (a partir de las 12 p.m.)

Good evening /gʊd 'iːvnɪŋ/ Buenas tardes (a partir de las 6 p.m.)

Good morning /gʊd 'mɔːnɪŋ/ Buenos días

good-looking /gʊd'lʊkɪŋ/ guapo/a

grandchild /'græntʃaɪld/ nieto/a

grandchildren /græn'tʃɪldrən/ nietos

grandfather /'grænfɑːðə/ abuelo

grandmother /'grænmʌðə/ abuela

grandparents /'grænpeərənts/ abuelos

great /greɪt/ genial; gran, grande

green /griːn/ verde

grey /greɪ/ gris

H

hair /heə/ pelo

hair and beauty salon /heə ənd 'bjuːti sælɒn/ salón de belleza y peluquería

hamster /'hæmstə/ hámster

hand /hænd/ mano

happen /'hæpən/ ocurrir, suceder

happy /'hæpi/ feliz, contento/a

hard /hɑːd/ duro, mucho

have breakfast /hæv 'brekfəst/ desayunar

have dinner /hæv 'dɪnə/ cenar

have lunch /hæv 'lʌntʃ/ comer (mediodía)

have tea /hæv 'tiː/ tomar el té

head /hed/ cabeza

hear /hɪə/ escuchar, oír

hello, hi /he'ləʊ, haɪ/ hola

help (n) /help/ ayuda

help (v) /help/ ayudar

hit /hɪt/ golpear

homework /'həʊmwɜːk/ deberes

hospital /'hɒspɪtl/ hospital

house /haʊs/ casa

housekeeper /'haʊskiːpə/ gobernanta

husband /'hʌzbənd/ marido

I

I'm sorry /aɪm 'sɒri/ Lo siento

in style /ɪn 'staɪl/ a lo grande

interesting /'ɪntrəstɪŋ/ interesante

interview /'ɪntəvjuː/ entrevista

It's (five) o'clock /ɪts (faɪv) ə'klɒk/ Son las (cinco) en punto

It's half past (five) /ɪts 'hɑːf pɑːst (faɪv)/ Son las (cinco) y media

It's quarter past (five) /ɪts 'kwɔːtə pɑːst (faɪv)/ Son las (cinco) y cuarto

It's quarter to (five) /ɪts 'kwɔːtə tə (faɪv)/ Son las (cinco) menos cuarto

It's ten past (five) /ɪts 'ten pɑːst (faɪv)/ Son las (cinco) y diez

It's ten to (five) /ɪts 'ten tə (faɪv)/ Son las (cinco) menos diez

Italian /ɪ'tælɪən/ italiano/a

J

jacket /'dʒækɪt/ chaqueta

January /'dʒænjʊəri/ enero

job /dʒɒb/ trabajo

July /dʒʊ'laɪ/ julio

June /dʒuːn/ junio

just /dʒʌst/ sólo, solamente

K

kitchen /'kɪtʃn/ cocina

kitten /'kɪtn/ gatito/a

L

lamp /læmp/ lámpara de pie o de mesa

language /'læŋgwɪdʒ/ lengua, idioma

late /leɪt/ tarde, hasta tarde

leg /leg/ pierna

letter /'letə/ carta

library /'laɪbrəri/ biblioteca

like /laɪk/ gustar

live /lɪv/ vivir

living room /'lɪvɪŋ ruːm/ salón, sala de estar

long /lɒŋ/ largo/a

look /lʊk/ mirar

love /lʌv/ encantar

M

March /mɑːtʃ/ marzo

married /'mærid/ casado/a

May /meɪ/ mayo

meal /miːl/ comida

meet /miːt/ conocer (a alguien); quedar / reunirse con

midday /mɪd'deɪ/ mediodía

middle-aged /mɪdl'eɪdʒd/ de mediana edad

midnight /'mɪdnaɪt/ medianoche

Monday /'mʌndeɪ/ lunes

mother /'mʌðə/ madre

mouth /maʊθ/ boca

N

nationality /næʃə'næləti/ nacionalidad

nearly /'nɪəli/ casi

need /niːd/ necesitar

never /'nevə/ nunca

new /njuː/ nuevo/a

nice /naɪs/ bonito/a; agradable

Nice to meet you /naɪs tə 'miːt juː/ Encantado/a de conocerte / conocerle

Nigeria /naɪ'dʒɪəriə/ Nigeria

Nigerian /naɪ'dʒɪəriən/ nigeriano/a

nine /naɪn/ nueve

nineteen /naɪn'tiːn/ diecinueve

ninety /'naɪnti/ noventa

ninth /naɪnθ/ noveno/a

noisy /'nɔɪzi/ ruidoso/a

nose /nəʊz/ nariz

notebook /'nəʊtbʊk/ cuaderno

nothing /'nʌθɪŋ/ nada

nought /nɔːt/ cero

November /nəʊ'vembə/ noviembre

now /naʊ/ ahora

O

October /ɒk'təʊbə/ octubre

often /'ɒfn/ a menudo

oh /əʊ/ cero

old /əʊld/ viejo/a, anciano/a

on holiday /ɒn 'hɒlədeɪ/ de vacaciones

on my way /ɒn maɪ 'weɪ/ en / de camino

one /wʌn/ uno/a

one hundred /wʌn 'hʌndrəd/ cien

orange /'ɒrɪndʒ/ naranja

outside /aʊt'saɪd/ fuera

P

parents /'peərənts/ padres

partner /'pɑːtnə/ compañero/a

party /'pɑːti/ fiesta

pen /pen/ bolígrafo

pence /pens/ peniques

pencil /'pensl/ lápiz

perform /pə'fɔːm/ tocar, actuar

pet /pet/ mascota

picture /'pɪktʃə/ foto; dibujo

pink /pɪŋk/ rosa

pitch /pɪtʃ/ campo, cancha

place /pleɪs/ lugar

play /pleɪ/ tocar; jugar

popcorn /'pɒpkɔːn/ palomitas de maíz

porter /'pɔːtə/ botones

post office /'pəʊst ɒfɪs/ oficina de correos

poster /'pəʊstə/ póster

pound /paʊnd/ libra (moneda)

practise /'præktɪs/ ensayar

problem /'prɒbləm/ problema

puppy /'pʌpi/ cachorro/a

purple /'pɜːpl/ morado/a

Q

quiet /'kwaɪət/ callado/a (*be ~!*: ¡cállate!)

R

rabbit /'ræbɪt/ conejo/a

read /riːd/ leer

Really? /'rɪəliː/ ¿De verdad?

receptionist /rɪ'sepʃənɪst/ recepcionista

red /red/ rojo/a

registration /redʒɪ'streɪʃn/ matrícula, inscripción

right now /raɪt 'naʊ/ ahora mismo

rock group /'rɒk gruːp/ grupo de *rock*

royal /'rɔɪəl/ real

rug /rʌg/ alfombra

run (n) /rʌn/ carrera

run (v) /rʌn/ correr

S

sad /sæd/ triste

Saturday /'sætədeɪ/ sábado

sausage /'sɒsɪdʒ/ salchicha

schoolbag /'skuːlbæg/ mochila

second /'sekənd/ segundo/a

sell /sel/ vender

September /sep'tembə/ septiembre

seven /'sevn/ siete

seventeen /sevn'tiːn/ diecisiete

seventh /'sevnθ/ séptimo/a

seventy /'sevnti/ setenta

shop assistant /'ʃɒp ə'sɪstənt/ dependiente/a de una tienda

short /ʃɔ:t/ corto/a; bajo/a

shower /'ʃaʊə/ ducha

sing /sɪŋ/ cantar

singer /'sɪŋə/ cantante

sister /'sɪstə/ hermana

six /sɪks/ seis

sixteen /sɪks'ti:n/ dieciséis

sixth /sɪksθ/ sexto/a

sixty /'sɪksti/ sesenta

sleep /sli:p/ dormir

slow /sləʊ/ lento/a

small /smɔ:l/ pequeño/a

snake /sneɪk/ serpiente

sofa /'səʊfə/ sofá

sometimes /'sʌmtaɪmz/ algunas veces, a veces

son /sʌn/ hijo

Sorry /'sɒri/ Lo siento

Spain /speɪn/ España

Spanish /'spænɪʃ/ español/a

speak /spi:k/ hablar

spend /spend/ gastar

square /skweə/ cuadrado/s

stamp /stæmp/ sello

start school /stɑ:t 'sku:l/ entrar a clase

study /'stʌdi/ estudiar

Sunday /'sʌndeɪ/ domingo

surgery /'sɜ:dʒəri/ consulta (del médico)

T

table /'teɪbəl/ mesa

take-away /'teɪkəweɪ/ para llevar

tall /tɔ:l/ alto/a

teach /ti:tʃ/ enseñar

teacher /'ti:tʃə/ profesor/a

team /ti:m/ equipo

ten /ten/ diez

tenth /tenθ/ décimo/a

thin /θɪn/ delgado/a

third /θɜ:d/ tercero/a

thirteen /θɜ:'ti:n/ trece

thirty /'θɜ:ti/ treinta

three /θri:/ tres

throw /θrəʊ/ lanzar, tirar

Thursday /'θɜ:zdeɪ/ jueves

tired /'taɪəd/ cansado/a

toast /təʊst/ tostada

today /tə'deɪ/ hoy

toe /təʊ/ dedo del pie

toilet /'tɔɪlət/ aseo, retrete

tonight /tə'naɪt/ esta noche

too /tu:/ también

Tuesday /'tju:zdeɪ/ martes

Turkey /'tɜ:ki/ Turquía

Turkish /'tɜ:kɪʃ/ turco/a

twelfth /twelfθ/ duodécimo/a

twelve /twelv/ doce

twenty /'twenti/ veinte

two /tu:/ dos

U

ugly /'ʌgli/ feo/a

uncle /'ʌnkl/ tío

usually /'ju:ʒʊəli/ normalmente

V

very /'veri/ muy

W

wait /weɪt/ esperar

waiter /'weɪtə/ camarero

wake up /weɪk 'ʌp/ despertar(se)

watch /wɒtʃ/ ver, observar

Wednesday /'wenzdeɪ/ miércoles

weekend /wi:k'end/ fin de semana

Welcome /'welkəm/ Bienvenido/a

What about you? /wɒt əbaʊt 'ju:/ ¿Y tú?

What's new? /wɒts 'nju:/ ¿Qué tal?, ¿Qué hay?

What's wrong? /wɒts 'rɒŋ/ ¿Qué pasa?, ¿Qué ocurre?

white /waɪt/ blanco/a

wife /waɪf/ esposa

win /wɪn/ ganar

write /raɪt/ escribir

Y

yellow /'jeləʊ/ amarillo/a

young /jʌŋ/ joven

Z

zero /'zɪərəʊ/ cero

USEFUL WORDS AND EXPRESSIONS

NUMBERS	NÚMEROS
nought / oh	cero
one	uno
two	dos
three	tres
four	cuatro
five	cinco
six	seis
seven	siete
eight	ocho
nine	nueve
ten	diez
eleven	once
twelve	doce
thirteen	trece
fourteen	catorce
fifteen	quince
sixteen	dieciséis
seventeen	diecisiete
eighteen	dieciocho
nineteen	diecinueve
twenty	veinte
twenty-one	veintiuno
twenty-two	veintidós
twenty-three	veintitrés
twenty-four	veinticuatro
twenty-five	veinticinco
twenty-six	veintiséis
twenty-seven	veintisiete
twenty-eight	veintiocho
twenty-nine	veintinueve
thirty	treinta
thirty-five	treinta y cinco
forty	cuarenta
forty-five	cuarenta y cinco
fifty	cincuenta
fifty-five	cincuenta y cinco
sixty	sesenta
sixty-five	sesenta y cinco
seventy	setenta
seventy-five	setenta y cinco
eighty	ochenta
eighty-five	ochenta y cinco
ninety	noventa
ninety-five	noventa y cinco
one hundred	cien

ORDINAL NUMBERS	NÚMEROS ORDINALES
first	primero
second	segundo
third	tercero
fourth	cuarto
fifth	quinto
sixth	sexto
seventh	séptimo
eighth	octavo
ninth	noveno
tenth	décimo
eleventh	undécimo
twelfth	duodécimo

THE TIME / TIME EXPRESSIONS	LA HORA / EXPRESIONES TEMPORALES
o'clock	en punto
ten past five	las cinco y diez
ten to	menos diez
quarter past	y cuarto
quarter to	menos cuarto
half past	y media
midday	mediodía
midnight	medianoche
in the morning	por la mañana
in the afternoon	por la tarde
in the evening	por la tarde
at night	por la noche
early	pronto, temprano
late	tarde, hasta tarde

DAYS OF THE WEEK	DÍAS DE LA SEMANA
Monday	lunes
Tuesday	martes
Wednesday	miércoles
Thursday	jueves
Friday	viernes
Saturday	sábado
Sunday	domingo

MONTHS	MESES
January	enero
February	febrero
March	marzo
April	abril
May	mayo
June	junio
July	julio
August	agosto
September	septiembre
October	octubre
November	noviembre
December	diciembre

Let's Go! 1 Student's Book

by Melissa Kendall

Burlington Books
P.O. Box 54411
3721 Limassol
Cyprus
Burlington Books is an imprint of Danos Books Ltd.

The publisher gratefully acknowledges the following for providing photographs:
AP: page 13 (Banderas); ASAP/Alamy: pages 60 (5); ASAP/Rex: page 31 (Royal Family); © Brand X Pictures: pages 7 (hamburger), 53 (fish and chips, tea cup), 97 (popcorn) 101 (g); © Corbis: pages 57 (sing, watch), 60 (cinema), 81, 83; © Digital Vision: page 52 (have tea), 71 (girl) 101 (a); © Dynamic Graphics Inc.: page 28 (family); © Getty Images / PhotoDisc: pages 7 (bus, telephone, taxi, passport), 12 (pencil, blackboard, desk, open book), 16 (3, 5, 6), 19 (open book, desk), 25 (Edward, Jill, Kate, Mavis), 31 (couple), 35 (cat, dog, hamster, kitten, puppy), 38 (cat, hamster, kitten, rabbit), 53 (breakfast), 57 (write), 60 (hospital, library, shop), 63 (couple), 68 (boring), 69 (cricket bat), 73 (blackboard, desk, dictionary, pen, pencil), 77 (f), 78, 81 (ex 2), 65; © Image 100: pages 66 (football), 71 (rugby); Image Bank / Getty Images: pages 13 (1, 3, 4, 6), 37 (1, 2, 3, 5); © Imagestate: pages 35 (fish), 38 (fish), 65 (help), 68 (quiet); © Image Source Ltd.: page 65 (play); © Ingram Publishing: pages 9 (pen), 12 (notebook, pen), 19 (pen), 28 (girl), 38 (snake), 53 (man), 73 (notebook), 97 (8); © Photos.com / Jupiter Images: pages 12 (chair), 16 (waiter, shop assistant, doctor, receptionist), 19 (chair), 23 (all except Indian male), 25 (Andrew, Lisa, Tim), 29 (clown, eyes, hair), 35 (rabbit, snake), 39 (couple), 43, 45, 47, 49, 52 (have breakfast, have dinner, have lunch), 55 (couple), 57 (cook, play), 61, 63 (mobile phone), 65 (clean, run, sleep, wait), 68 (fast, happy, interesting, noisy, sad), 69 (playing cricket), 71 (boy with mobile phone), 73 (chair), 77 (a, b, e, g, h), 81 (boy with football), 101 (h); © RubberBall Productions: pages 47, 55, 57 (dance) 60 (6); © Shutterstock.com: pages 7 (ambulance, hotel), 21 (ex B), 23 (Indian male), 25 (Mark), 39 (cats), 55 (food), 60 (bank, cake), 63 (shopping), 65 (4), 77 (c, d), 78 (books), 101 (d, e); Wenn: pages 13 (5), 37 (4).

ISBN 978-9963-47-849-1

10 9 8 7 6 5 4 3 2 1
17 16 15 14 13 12 11 10 09 08